IN PRESS,

Prof. Davies' new Work on Mathematical Instruction.

THE

LOGIC AND UTITITY

OF

MATHEMATICS;

OR,

AN ANALYSIS OF THE PRINCIPLES OF THE SCIENCE—OF THE NATURE OF THE REASONING—AND OF THE BEST METHODS OF IMPARTING INSTRUCTION.

BY

CHARLES DAVIES, LL.D.

In the Logic and Utility of Mathematics, the principal subjects are analyzed in a manner similar to the analysis of Arithmetic in this work: and from that work, this has been mainly taken.

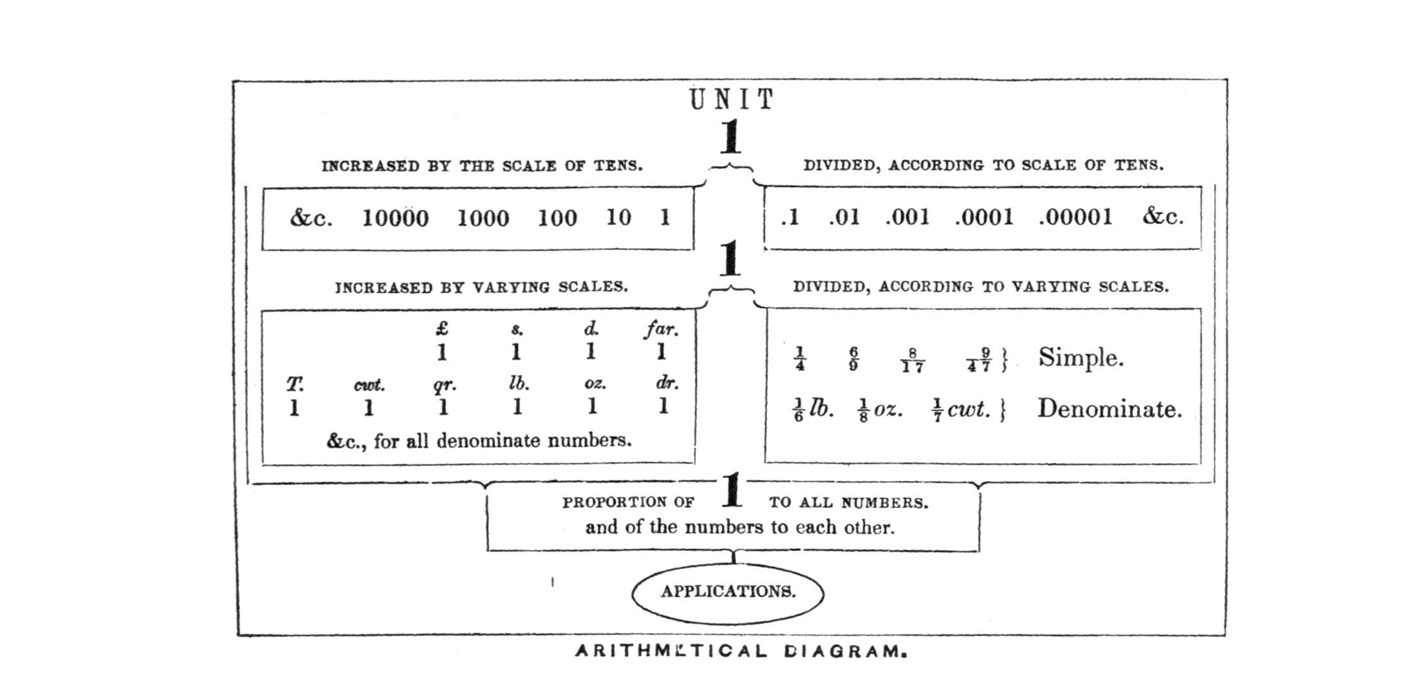

ARITHMETICAL DIAGRAM.

GRAMMAR

OF

ARITHMETIC;

OR,

AN ANALYSIS

OF THE

LANGUAGE OF FIGURES AND SCIENCE OF NUMBERS.

BY

CHARLES DAVIES, LL.D.,

AUTHOR OF FIRST LESSONS IN ARITHMETIC; SCHOOL ARITHMETIC; LOGIC AND UTILITY OF MATHEMATICS; UNIVERSITY ARITHMETIC; ELEMENTARY ALGEBRA; ELEMENTARY GEOMETRY: ELEMENTS OF DRAWING AND MENSURATION; ELEMENTS OF SURVEYING; ELEMENTS OF ANALYTICAL GEOMETRY; DESCRIPTIVE GEOMETRY; SHADES, SHADOWS, AND LINEAR PERSPECTIVE; AND DIFFERENTIAL AND INTEGRAL CALCULUS.

NEW YORK:
PUBLISHED BY A. S. BARNES & CO.,
NO. 51 JOHN-STREET.

CINCINNATI:—H. W. DERBY & CO.
1850.

TO TEACHERS.

WILL you spare a little time from your responsible and laborious duties, to read a few pages addressed to you by one of your own number who has spent over a third of a century in the business of teaching; and that, too, in the single subject of mathematical science, of which arithmetic, though the elementary, is nevertheless one of the most important branches.

I wish to give you the results of a very full and careful analysis, both of the Science and Art of Arithmetic, and to offer you some suggestions on the best methods of imparting instruction.

Is not the subject, to which I ask your attention, of such importance as to demand a careful and candid examination? Do not the interests of education and science, dependent as they are on the methods of teaching, lay you under obligations to look carefully into those systems of instruction presented for your consideration? And is not this duty especially obligatory, when the subject is one that not only lays in the mind the foundations of true science, but also develops those rules of art which regulate nearly all the affairs of civilized life?

If we cannot obtain such an examination from the Teachers, from whom are we to expect it? The lawyer leaves his home at an early hour, and toils through the day over his cases and books. The merchant is in his counting-room: the physician visiting his patients: the manufacturer at his workshop: and the farmer in his field. Thus, the whole interests of education are committed to those who are appointed to instruct the young; and to you, must we mainly look, for that intellectual and moral development which is the glory of a free people, and the only sure foundation of Free Institutions.

With this appreciation of the importance and dignity of your vocation, I lay before you, with profound respect and much diffidence, a plan for giving instruction in arithmetic. I cannot ask you to approve it; for that must be an act of your judgment. I do not ask you to favor it; for, as educators, you must be impartial. I do not ask you to introduce and use it; for, if there be one duty more sacred than another, it is that of selecting books for the instruction of the young. I therefore merely ask you to *examine*—to scrutinize it—to see if it be founded on right principles—and then to decide, whether on the whole it is likely to aid in the two objects of a scientific education: viz.

1st. To establish habits of quick, accurate, and profound thought; and

2dly. To give skill in the application of principles in all the practical departments and business of life.

These two objects should be kept constantly before the minds of educators. *It is the power of thought which stretches out the horizon of the mind—It is the skill of applying principles which gives practical value to all knowledge.*

Arithmetic is the first subject presented to the mind of a child, in which he is required to abstract ideas from the sensible objects from which he derives them. You say to John, Charles has two apples and William three; how many have both of them? He answers, Five—meaning five apples—for, he understands the phrase, "how many?" to apply to apples. Then put to him the corresponding abstract question, Two and three are how many? and the question is one of an entirely different character. It is, in this form, a question, the true answer to which, requires the exercise of the faculties of abstraction and generalization. The ideas of two and three are abstract—that is, entirely disconnected with sensible objects, and they are imperfect until generalized—that is, until the mind sees that the terms two, and three, and five, are applicable to any things whatever.

You teach John the meaning of the words, one, two, three, four, five, &c., and illustrate these meanings by means of sensible objects, and you give him distinct notions not only of the words, as connected with things, but also of the abstract terms by which the number of those things is expressed. As soon as the terms become familiar, the faculties of judgment and reasoning are brought into exercise and development. Thus, at a very early period, these great faculties of the mind, apprehension, judgment, and the reasoning powers, are put in action: and how important to the future development of the mind that they be rightly directed and properly trained!

How, then, should the subject of Arithmetic be presented?

1st. By presenting the elements separately;

2d. By presenting them in their natural order, and pointing out the relations between them; and

3dly. By deducing from the principles of the science all the rules of application, and then illustrating the various ways in which they are applied.

Looking at the Arithmetical Diagram, which faces the title-page, you will see an exact map of the subject. The UNIT 1, at the top, is the basis of the plan, as it is, certainly, the basis of all numbers. Then, are derived from it, the integer numbers on the left. First, the Simple Numbers, in which the units increase according to the scale of tens; and then the Denominate Numbers, in which the units increase according to varying scales.

On the right are the Fractions. First, the Decimal Fractions, in which the units, in passing from unity, decrease according to the scale of tens; and second, the Common or Vulgar Fractions, in which the unit is divided arbitrarily; that is, according to varying scales.

Next comes the subject of Proportion; that is, an examination of the relations which exist between the unit 1 and all the numbers which come from it, whether Integer or Fractional, Simple or Denominate; and then the relations of these numbers with each other. These three heads embrace the elementary science of Numbers. Their applications come next in order.

Now, it would seem of consequence that the impression be given early, that Arithmetic has but one elementary idea—the idea of the UNIT 1; and that every other thought is connected with this thought, and every other number with this number.

Regarding the subject from this point of view, the learner sees all the integer numbers flow out from the unit 1. Varying the process a little, he sees all the fractions flowing from the same source. Wishing to compare these numbers with each other, he finds that he must, in effect, first compare them with the unit 1. He thus finds that the unit 1, which is the basis of all numbers, is also the basis of all arithmetical operations.

Having thus understood the properties and relations of numbers, the learner finds no difficulty in their application, and is thus led to regard Arithmetic in its true light; viz. as a science and an art: the former developing its principles and pointing out their connection—the latter applying them.

This manner of presenting the subject of arithmetic causes the learner to look at it from *within*—to see and consider its structure, and to analyze every part, as the system of reasoning is gradually developed. When so trained, the learner looks back and contemplates all the steps of his progress, with their connections and relations. You have taken him to the first thought. You have shown him the little spring that is the source of a mighty river; and as he traces it along and finds new rills flowing into it, he will not be unmindful of its origin. He will classify and arrange all new impressions; he will divide and analyze; he will combine and generalize, and that dark cloud which envelops the subject of numbers will pass away before the sunlight of science.

It is to the shame of science that it has yet presented no acceptable plan of treating the subject of Arithmetic—that the technical terms are yet unsettled—that we are yet divided in opinion even in regard to a correct definition of addition.*

As regards the arrangement of subjects, Fancy rather than Science seems to have presided over this department. Even in the late treatises, authors appear to have studied diversity rather than agreement.

We find the twin sisters, Vulgar and Decimal Fractions, separated by the entire class of Denominate Numbers; and the Rule of Three, that great analyzer of numbers, which used to be called the Golden Rule, in compliment to its great practical utility, arranged after most of the practical rules, as though it were, in future, to be stowed away among the old lumber of a garret. Such a diversity of methods confuses both teacher and learner, and operates as a nightmare on the progress of education.†

Having sketched the general outline of the plan, I would now call your attention to the means employed to bring the mind into closer connection with the thoughts. These means are the adoption of a more

* Art. 100. † Art. 85.

brief and perspicuous language. You will find this language for Addition, fully explained in the articles from 10 to 16 inclusive; for Subtraction, in article 17; for Multiplication, in article 19; and for Division, in article 20. You will also find the language of numbers much dwelt upon, throughout the entire analysis.

In developing the analysis, it seemed to me, that one of the greatest difficulties in the study of Arithmetic, had arisen from a want of knowledge of the language in which the ideas, that constitute the science, are expressed and communicated.

We find but ten characters in the arithmetical alphabet, and but four hundred and eighty-eight elementary combinations.* We also find that there are but three general ways of combining any two of the characters with each other, so as to give them different significations.† Now, a language so simple can be easily and well learned in a short time. But instead of learning it, as a language, and then using it, as a means of expressing ideas and communicating thoughts, we plunge the learner into the *principles* of the science, without the aid of its language, or without pausing to consider how poorly he may be prepared to comprehend, arrange, and classify its abstract ideas.

The fact, that we have spelled all the words of the arithmetical language, instead of reading them,—that we have paid no attention whatever to the language, as such,—that there has been no settled arrangement of the subjects, and that a pupil, in the course of a

* Art. 94. † Art. 96.

school education, is probably put into half a dozen systems—may, in some measure, account for the time which is wasted, and the perplexities endured, in the study of Arithmetic.

If you shall deem the Grammar worthy of study, as a class-book, it should be studied in connection with an arithmetic of the second grade, about the place where you would teach the grammar of any other language, and one month will suffice to teach it thoroughly. If you do not deem it worthy of this honor, you may, perhaps, in your leisure moments, chalk out the Arithmetical Diagram on the blackboard, and explain its parts and connections. Even if this do not strike you favorably, you will possibly find some thoughts or suggestions which you can make available in your teachings.

In conclusion, Teachers, permit me to add, that I did not feel myself at liberty to complain of a grievance without offering a remedy. I have, therefore, presented you a plan which has UNITY for its basis, UNITY in its design, and UNITY in its execution. The plan, if followed, will give great facility in the practical use of figures, and will open the minds of your pupils to a clear apprehension of the first principles of mathematical science. It is respectfully submitted for your consideration.

I am, very respectfully,

Your friend and obt. servant,

CHARLES DAVIES.

CONTENTS.

SECTION I.

SECTION II.

SECTION III.

SECTION IV.

SECTION V.

GRAMMAR OF ARITHMETIC.

SECTION I.

INTEGER UNITS.

First Notions of Numbers.

1. There is but a single elementary idea in the science of numbers: it is the idea of the UNIT ONE. There is but one way of impressing this idea on the mind. It is by presenting to the senses a single object; as, one apple, one peach, one pear, &c.

2. There are three signs by means of which the idea of one is expressed and communicated. They are,

1st. By the word ONE.

2d. By the Roman character I.

3d. By the figure 1.

---

1. How many elementary ideas are there in numbers? What is that idea? How many ways are there of impressing this idea on the mind? What is that way?

2. How many signs are there of one? What are they?

3. If one be added to one, the idea thus arising is different from the idea of one, and is complex. This new idea has also three signs; viz. TWO, II., and 2. If one be again added, that is, added to two, the new idea has likewise three signs; viz. THREE, III., and 3. The expressions for these, and similar ideas, are called numbers; hence,

NUMBERS *are expressions for one or more things of the same kind.*

Ideas of Numbers generalized.

4. If we begin with the idea of the number one, and then add it to one, making two; and then add it to two, making three; and then to three, making four; and then to four, making five, and so on; it is plain that we shall form a series of numbers, each of which will be greater by one than that which precedes it. Now, one, or

---

3. If one be added to itself, is the idea thus arising different from that of one? Is it a simple or complex idea? How many signs has this new idea? What are they? What are the expressions for such ideas called? What then are numbers?

4. If one be added to one, and then in succession to the numbers which follow, what is formed? What is the basis of this series of numbers?

unity, is the basis of this series of numbers, and each number may be expressed in three ways:

1st. By the words ONE, TWO, THREE, &c. of our common language;

2d. By the Roman characters; and

3d. By figures.

5. Since all numbers, whether integer or fractional, must come from, and hence be connected with, the unit one, it follows that there is but one purely elementary idea in the science of numbers. Hence, the idea of every number, regarded as made up of units, (and all numbers except one must be so regarded when we analyze them,) is necessarily complex. For, since the number arises from the addition of ones the apprehension of it is incomplete until we understand how those additions were made; and therefore, a full idea of the number is necessarily complex.

6. But if we regard a number as an entirety,

In how many ways may each number be expressed? What are those ways?

5. From what are all numbers derived? How many elementary ideas are there in the science of numbers? What is that idea? Is the idea of any number other than unity, complex or incomplex? Why is it complex?

that is, as an entire or whole thing, as an entire two, or three, or four, without pausing to analyze the units of which it is made up, it may then be regarded as a simple or incomplex idea; though, as we have seen, such idea may always be traced to that of the unit one, which forms the basis of the number.

Unity and a Unit defined.

7. When we name a number, as twenty feet, two things are necessary to its clear apprehension.

1st. A distinct apprehension of the *single thing* which forms the basis of the number; and

2d. A distinct apprehension of the *number of times* which that thing is taken.

The single thing, which forms the basis of the number, is called UNITY, or a UNIT. It is called unity, when it is regarded as the *primary basis* of the number; that is, when it is the final standard to which all the numbers that come from it

---

6. In what sense may the idea of a number be regarded as incomplex? If we analyze the number, what do we find to be its basis?

7. When we name a number, how many things are necessary to its full apprehension? What are those things?

are referred. It is called a unit when it is regarded as one of the collection of several equal things which form a number. Thus, in the example, one foot, regarded as a standard and the basis of the number, is called UNITY; but, considered as one of the twenty equal feet which make up the number, it is called a UNIT.

Of Simple and Denominate Numbers.

8. A simple or abstract unit, is ONE, without regard to the kind of thing to which the term one may be applied.

A denominate or concrete unit, is *one thing* named or denominated; as, one apple, one peach, one pear, one horse, &c.

9. A number whose unit is simple or abstract, is called a simple or abstract number; and a number whose unit is named, is called a denominate number. Thus, fifteen is a simple number,

---

What is the single thing called which forms the basis of the number? When is it called unity? When is it called a unit? In the number twenty feet, when is one foot unity and when a unit?

8. What is a simple or abstract unit? What is a denominate or concrete unit?

9. What is a number called whose unit is simple or abstract? What is a number called whose unit is named?

because the unit is *one;* and fifteen pounds is a denominate number, because its unit, one pound, is denominated or named.

Alphabet—Words—Grammar.

10. The term alphabet, in its most general sense, denotes a set of characters which form the elements of a written language.

When any one of these characters, or any combination of them, is used as the sign of a distinct notion or idea, it is called a word; and the naming of the characters of which the word is composed, is called its spelling.

Grammar, as a science, treats of the established connection between words as the signs of ideas.

Arithmetical Alphabet.

11. The arithmetical alphabet consists of ten characters, called figures. They are,

Naught,	One,	Two,	Three,	Four,	Five,	Six,	Seven,	Eight,	Nine.
0	1	2	3	4	5	6	7	8	9

10. What do you understand by the term alphabet? What is a word? What is the spelling of a word? What is grammar?

11. Of how many characters does the arithmetical alphabet consist? What are their names?

and each may be regarded as a word, since it stands for a distinct idea.

Words—Spelling and Reading in Addition.

12. The idea of one, being elementary, the character 1 which represents it, is also elementary, and hence, cannot be spelled by the other characters of the Arithmetical Alphabet (Art. 11). But the idea which is expressed by 2 comes from the addition of 1 and 1: hence, the word represented by the character 2, may be spelled by 1 and 1. Thus, 1 and 1 are 2, is the arithmetical spelling of the word two.

Three is spelled thus: 1 and 2 are 3; and also, 2 and 1 are 3.

Four is spelled, 1 and 3 are 4; 3 and 1 are 4; 2 and 2 are 4.

Five is spelled, 1 and 4 are 5; 4 and 1 are 5; 2 and 3 are 5; 3 and 2 are 5.

Six is spelled, 1 and 5 are 6; 5 and 1 are 6; 2 and 4 are 6; 4 and 2 are 6; 3 and 3 are 6.

May each be regarded as a word? Why?

12. Can one be spelled by the other characters of the arithmetical alphabet? What is the arithmetical spelling of two? What of three? What are the spellings of four? Of five?

13. In a similar manner, any number in arithmetic may be spelled; and hence we see that the process of spelling in addition consists simply, in naming any two elements which will make up the number. All the numbers in addition are therefore spelled with two syllables. The *reading* consists in naming only the word which expresses the final idea. Thus,

0	1	2	3	4	5	6	7	8	9
1	1	1	1	1	1	1	1	1	1
One	two	three	four	five	six	seven	eight	nine	ten.

We may now read the words which express the first hundred combinations.

READINGS.

1	2	3	4	5	6	7	8	9	10
1	1	1	1	1	1	1	1	1	1

1	2	3	4	5	6	7	8	9	10
2	2	2	2	2	2	2	2	2	2

1	2	3	4	5	6	7	8	9	10
3	3	3	3	3	3	3	3	3	3

13. What is the process of spelling in addition? How many syllables are used in arithmetical spelling? What is the reading? What is the difference between reading and spelling?

1	2	3	4	5	6	7	8	9	10
4	4	4	4	4	4	4	4	4	4
1	2	3	4	5	6	7	8	9	10
5	5	5	5	5	5	5	5	5	5
1	2	3	4	5	6	7	8	9	10
6	6	6	6	6	6	6	6	6	6
1	2	3	4	5	6	7	8	9	10
7	7	7	7	7	7	7	7	7	7
1	2	3	4	5	6	7	8	9	10
8	8	8	8	8	8	8	8	8	8
1	2	3	4	5	6	7	8	9	10
9	9	9	9	9	9	9	9	9	9
1	2	3	4	5	6	7	8	9	10
10	10	10	10	10	10	10	10	10	10

14. In this example, beginning at the right hand, we say, 8, 17, 18, 26: setting down the 6 and carrying the 2, we say, 8, 13, 20, 22, 29: setting down the 9 and carrying the 2, we say, 9, 12, 18,

```
 878
 421
 679
 354
 764
----
3096
```

14. How do you go through the process of addition by reading the figures? Give an example of this method.

22, 30: and setting down the 30, we have the entire sum 3096. All the examples in addition may be done in a similar manner.

15. The advantages of this method of reading over spelling are very great.

1st. The mind acquires ideas more readily through the eye than through either of the other senses. Hence, if the mind be taught to apprehend the result of a combination, by merely seeing its elements, the process of arriving at it is much shorter than when those elements are presented through the instrumentality of sound. Thus, to *see* 4 and 4, and *think* 8, is a very different thing from saying, four and four are eight.

2d. The mind operates with greater rapidity and certainty, the nearer it is brought to the ideas which it is to apprehend and combine. Therefore, all unnecessary words load it and impede its operations. Hence, to spell when we can read, is to fill the mind with words and sounds, instead of ideas.

3d. All the operations of arithmetic, beyond the elementary combinations, are performed on

15. Does the method of reading possess any advantages over the method of spelling? What is the first advantage named? What is the second? What the third?

paper; and if rapidly and accurately done, must be done through the eye and by reading. Hence, the great importance of beginning early with a method which must be acquired before any considerable skill can be attained in the use of figures.

REMARKS.

16. It must not be supposed that the *reading* can be accomplished until the *spelling* has first been learned.

In our common language, we first learn the alphabet, then we pronounce each letter in a word, and finally, we pronounce the word. We should do the same in the arithmetical reading.

Words—Spelling and Reading in Subtraction.

17. The processes of spelling and reading which we have explained in the addition of numbers, may, with slight modifications, be ap-

---

16. Which is first learned, the arithmetical reading or spelling? How is it in our common language? What is the process in learning a word?

17. May the method of reading numbers, explained for addition, be also used in subtraction? Give an example of a reading in subtraction. What is the general method of reading in subtraction?

plied in subtraction. Thus, if we are to subtract 2 from 5, we say, ordinarily, 2 from 5 leaves 3; or 2 from 5 three remains. Now, the word, three, is suggested by the relation in which 2 and 5 stand to each other, and this word may be read at once. Hence, *the reading, in subtraction, is simply naming the word, which expresses the difference between the subtrahend and minuend.* Thus, we may read each word of the following one hundred combinations.

READINGS.

1	2	3	4	5	6	7	8	9	10
1	1	1	1	1	1	1	1	1	1
2	3	4	5	6	7	8	9	10	11
2	2	2	2	2	2	2	2	2	2
3	4	5	6	7	8	9	10	11	12
3	3	3	3	3	3	3	3	3	3
4	5	6	7	8	9	10	11	12	13
4	4	4	4	4	4	4	4	4	4
5	6	7	8	9	10	11	12	13	14
5	5	5	5	5	5	5	5	5	5
6	7	8	9	10	11	12	13	14	15
6	6	6	6	6	6	6	6	6	6

7	8	9	10	11	12	13	14	15	16
7	7	7	7	7	7	7	7	7	7

8	9	10	11	12	13	14	15	16	17
8	8	8	8	8	8	8	8	8	8

9	10	11	12	13	14	15	16	17	18
9	9	9	9	9	9	9	9	9	9

10	11	12	13	14	15	16	17	18	19
10	10	10	10	10	10	10	10	10	10

REMARK.

18. It should be remarked, that in subtraction, as well as in addition, the spelling of the words must necessarily precede their reading. The spelling consists in naming the figures with which the operation is performed, the steps of the operation, and the final result. The reading consists in naming the final result only.

Spelling and Reading in Multiplication

19. Spelling in multiplication is similar to the corresponding process in addition or subtraction. It is simply naming the two elements which pro-

18. Does the spelling of the words in subtraction precede their reading? In what does the spelling consist? In what does the reading consist?

duce the product; whilst the reading consists in naming only the word which expresses the final result.

In multiplying each number from 1 to 10 by 2, we usually say, two times 1 are 2; two times 3 are 6; two times 4 are 8; two times 5 are 10; two times 6 are 12; two times 7 are 14; two times 8 are 16; two times 9 are 18; two times 10 are 20. Whereas, we should merely read, and say, 2, 4, 6, 8, 10, 12, 14, 16, 18, 20.

In a similar manner we read the entire multiplication table.

READINGS.

12	11	10	9	8	7	6	5	4	3	2	1
											1

12	11	10	9	8	7	6	5	4	3	2	1
											2

12	11	10	9	8	7	6	5	4	3	2	1
											3

19. In what does the spelling in multiplication consist? In what does the reading consist? In multiplying each number from 1 to 10, by 2, what words do we generally use? What should we say? What other numbers may be similarly read?

12	11	10	9	8	7	6	5	4	3	2	1
											4

12	11	10	9	8	7	6	5	4	3	2	1
											5

12	11	10	9	8	7	6	5	4	3	2	1
											6

12	11	10	9	8	7	6	5	4	3	2	1
											7

12	11	10	9	8	7	6	5	4	3	2	1
											8

12	11	10	9	8	7	6	5	4	3	2	1
											9

12	11	10	9	8	7	6	5	4	3	2	1
											10

12	11	10	9	8	7	6	5	4	3	2	1
											11

12	11	10	9	8	7	6	5	4	3	2	1
											12

Spelling and Reading in Division.

20. In all the cases of short division, the quotient may be read immediately without naming the process by which it is obtained. Thus, in dividing the following numbers by 2, we merely read the words below.

2)4	6	8	10	12	16	18	22
two	three	four	five	six	eight	nine	eleven.

In a similar manner, all the words, expressing the results in short division, may be read.

READINGS.

2)2 4 6 8 10 12 14 16 18 20 22 24

3)3 6 9 12 15 18 21 24 27 30 33 36

4)4 8 12 16 20 24 28 32 36 40 44 48

5)5 10 15 20 25 30 35 40 45 50 55 60

6)6 12 18 24 30 36 42 48 54 60 66 72

7)7 14 21 28 35 42 49 56 63 70 77 84

---

20. How will you perform short division by the method of reading? Give an example of reading in short division.

8)	8	16	24	32	40	48	56	64	72	80	88	96
9)	9	18	27	36	45	54	63	72	81	90	99	108
10)	10	20	30	40	50	60	70	80	90	100	110	120
11)	11	22	33	44	55	66	77	88	99	110	121	132
12)	12	24	36	48	60	72	84	96	108	120	132	144

Units increasing by the Scale of Tens.

21. The idea of a particular number is necessarily complex; for, the mind naturally asks:

1st. What is the unit or basis of the number? and,

2d. How many times is the unit or basis taken?

22. A figure indicates how many times a unit is taken. Each of the ten figures, however written, or however placed, always expresses as many units as its name imports, and no more; nor does the *figure itself* at all indicate the kind of unit. Still, every number expressed by one

21. Is the idea of a particular number simple or complex? What must be known before the number can be apprehended?

or more figures, has for its basis either the abstract unit one, or a denominate unit (Art. 9) If a denominate unit, its value or kind is pointed out either by our common language, or as we shall presently see, by the *place* where the figure is written.

The *number* of units which may be expressed by either of the ten figures, is indicated by the name of the figure. If the figure stands alone, and the unit is not denominated, the basis of the number is the abstract unit 1.

23. If we write 0 on the right of 1, we have - - - - - - - - - - 10, which is read ONE ten. Here 1 still expresses ONE, but it is ONE ten; that is, a unit ten times as great as the unit 1; and this is called a unit of the *second order*.

---

22. What does a figure indicate? What, then, will each figure, however written, express? Does the figure indicate the kind of unit? What basis has every number, whether expressed by one or more figures? If a denominate unit, how is its value or kind pointed out? By what is the number of units, that may be expressed by either of the ten characters, indicated? If the figure stands alone, and the unit is not denominated, what is the basis of the number?

23. If a cipher be written on the right of 1, what will the 1 then express? What is this unit called?

Again; if we write two 0's on the right of 1, we have - - - - - - - 100,

which is read ONE hundred. Here again, 1 still expresses ONE, but it is ONE hundred; that is, a unit ten times as great as the unit ONE ten, and a hundred times as great as the unit 1.

24. If three 1's are written by the side of each other, thus - - - - 111,

the ideas, expressed in our common language, are these:

1st. *That the* 1 *on the right, will either express a single thing denominated, or the abstract unit one.*

2d. *That the* 1 *next at the left expresses* 1 *ten; that is, a unit ten times as great as the first.*

If we write two ciphers on the right of 1, what will 1 then express? What is it called? How many times as great, is it, as 1 ten? How many times as great as 1? If we write three ciphers on the right of 1, what will 1 then express? What is it called? How many times as great, is it, as 1 hundred? How many times as great as 1 ten? How many times as great as 1?

24. If three 1's are written by the side of each other, how will you express the ideas in our common language? Generally, when figures are written by the side of each other, what is the relation of their units? What, then, fixes the unit of a figure?

3d. *That the* 1 *still further to the left expresses* 1 *hundred; that is, a unit ten times as great as the second, and one hundred times as great as the first; and similarly if there were other places.*

When figures are thus written by the side of each other, the arithmetical language establishes a relation between the units of their places: that is, the unit of each place, as we pass from the right hand towards the left, increases according to the scale of tens. Therefore, by a law of the arithmetical language, *the place of a figure fixes its unit.*

If, then, we write a row of 0's as a scale, thus:

1 hundred billion,	1 ten billion,	1 billion,	1 hundred million,	1 ten million,	1 million,	1 hundred thousand,	1 ten thousand,	1 thousand,	1 hundred,	1 ten,	1 unit,
0	0	0,	0	0	0,	0	0	0,	0	0	0

the *unit of each place* is determined, as well as the *law* of change in passing from one place

What is the scale for writing numbers? What does this scale establish? What two things, then, would be necessary in order to express a number of units of any order?

to another. If, then, it were required to express a given number of units, of any order, we first select from the arithmetical alphabet the character which designates the number, and then write it in the place corresponding to the order. Thus, to express three millions, we write

3000000;

and similarly for all numbers.

25. It should be observed, that a figure being *a character which represents value*, can have no value in and of itself. The *number* of things, which any figure expresses, is determined by its name, as given in the arithmetical alphabet. The *kind* of thing, or unit of the figure, is fixed either by naming it, as in the case of a denominate number, or by the place which the figure occupies, when written by the side of or over* other figures.

The phrase "local value of a figure," so long in use, is, therefore, without signification when

* See Art. 96.

25. Is a figure a thing of value, or a representative of value? Can it have a value, in and of itself? What determines the number of the things which a figure expresses? What determines the kind of thing, or unit of the figure?

applied to a figure: the term "local value," being applicable to the *unit of the place*, and not to the figure which occupies the place.

26. Federal Money affords an example of a series of denominate units, increasing according to the scale of tens: thus,

Eagle,	Dollar,	Dime,	Cent,	Mill,
1	1	1	1	1

may be read 11 thousand 1 hundred and 11 *mills;* or, 1111 *cents* and 1 mill; or, 111 dimes 1 cent and 1 mill; or, 11 dollars 1 dime 1 cent and 1 mill; or, 1 eagle 1 dollar 1 dime 1 cent and 1 mill. Thus, we may read the number with either of its units as a basis, or we may name them all: thus, 1 eagle, 1 dollar, 1 dime, 1 cent, 1 mill. Generally, in Federal Money, we read in the denominations of dollars, cents, and mills; and should say, 11 dollars 11 cents and 1 mill.

Is the term "local value" applicable to a figure? To what is it applicable?

26. Are the units of Federal Money simple or denominate? According to what scale do they increase? Give all the readings of the example. How is Federal Money generally read?

27. Examples in reading figures:—

If we have the figures - - - - 89
we may read them by their smallest unit, and say eighty-nine; or, we may say 8 tens and 9 units.

Again, the figures - - - - - - - 567
may be read by the smallest unit; viz. five hundred and sixty-seven; or we may say, 56 tens and 7 units; or, 5 hundreds 6 tens and 7 units.

Again, the number expressed by - 74896
may be read, seventy-four thousand eight hundred and ninety-six. Or, it may be read, 7489 tens and 6 units; or, 748 hundreds 9 tens and 6 units; or, 74 thousands 8 hundreds 9 tens and 6 units; or, 7 ten thousands 4 thousands 8 hundreds 9 tens and 6 units; and we may read in a similar way all other numbers.

Although we should teach all the correct readings of a number, we should also teach, that it is generally most convenient in practice to read by the lowest unit of a number. Thus,

---

27. Give the different readings of 89. Give the different readings of 567. Give the different readings of 74896. By what unit is it generally most convenient to read a number?

in the numeration table, we read each period by the lowest unit of that period. For example, in the number

874,967,847,047,

we read 874 *billions* 967 *millions* 847 *thousands* and 47.

Units increasing according to Varying Scales.

28. If we write the well-known signs of the English money, and place 1 under each denomination, we shall have

£	*s.*	*d.*	*f.*
1	1	1	1.

Now, the signs £ *s. d.* and *f.* fix the value of the unit 1 in each denomination; and they also determine the relations which subsist between the different units. For example, this simple language expresses these ideas:

1st. That the unit of the right-hand place is 1 farthing—of the place next to the left, 1 penny

---

By what unit is each period read in the numeration table?

28. What two things are determined by the signs of pounds, shillings, pence, and farthings?

—of the next place, 1 shilling—of the next place, 1 pound; and

2d. That 4 units of the lowest denomination make one unit of the next higher; 12 of the second, one of the third; and 20 of the third, one of the fourth.

If we take the denominate numbers of the Avoirdupois weight, we have

Ton.	*cwt.*	*qr.*	*lb.*	*oz.*	*dr.*
1	1	1	1	1	1;

in which the units increase in the following manner: viz. the second unit, counting from the right, is sixteen times as great as the first: the third sixteen times as great as the second: the fourth twenty-five times as great as the third: the fifth four times as great as the fourth: and the sixth twenty times as great as the fifth. The scale, therefore, for this class of denominate numbers varies according to the above laws.

If we take any other class of denominate numbers, as the Troy weight, or any of the systems of measures, we shall have different

---

What ideas does this simple language express? Name the different degrees of the scale for the Avoirdupois weight? If we take another class of denominate numbers, will the degrees of the scale be the same or different?

scales for the formation of the different units. But in all the formations, we shall recognise the application of the same general principles.

There are, therefore, two general methods of forming the different systems of integer numbers from the unit one. The first consists in preserving a constant law of relation between the different unities: viz. that their values shall change according to the scale of tens. This gives the system of common numbers.

The second method consists in the application of known, though varying laws of change in the unities. These changes in the unities, produce the entire system of denominate numbers, each class of which has its appropriate scale, and the changes among the units of the same class are indicated by the different degrees of its scale.

Are the methods of forming the numbers the same in all the classes? How many *general* methods are there of forming the different systems of integer numbers? What is the first? To what system of numbers does this give rise? What is the second? To what system of numbers does this give rise?

Integer Units of Arithmetic.

29. There are four principal classes of units in arithmetic:

1st. Abstract, or simple units;
2d. Units of Currency;
3d. Units of Weight; and
4th Units of Measure.

First among the units of arithmetic stands the simple or abstract unit 1. This is the basis of all simple numbers, and becomes the basis, also, of all denominate numbers by merely naming, in succession, the particular things to which it is applied.

It is also the basis of all fractions. Merely as the unit 1, it is a whole which may be divided according to any law, forming every variety of fraction; and if we apply it to a particular thing, the fraction becomes denominate, and we have expressions for all conceivable parts of that thing.

29. How many principal classes are there of integer units? What are they? Which unit stands first among the units of arithmetic? Of what classes of integer numbers is it the basis? Of what other classes of numbers is it the basis?

30. It has been remarked, (Art. 7), that we can form no distinct apprehension of a number, until we have a clear notion of its unit, and the number of times the unit is taken. *The unit is the great basis.* The utmost care, therefore, should be taken to impress on the minds of learners, a clear and distinct idea of the actual value of the unit of every number with which they have to do. If it be a number expressing currency, one or more of the coins should be exhibited, and the value dwelt upon; after which, distinct notions of the other units can be acquired by comparison.

If the number be one of weight, some unit should be exhibited, as one pound, or one ounce, and an idea of its weight acquired by actually lifting it. This is the only way in which we can learn the true signification of the terms.

If the number be one of measure, either linear,

30. What two things are necessary in order to apprehend clearly what a number expresses? What is the great basis? What matter, therefore, in teaching, should receive special attention? When the number expresses currency, how should the value of the unit be impressed? If the number be one of weight, how should the idea of the unit be fixed in the mind?

superficial, liquid, or solid, its unit should also be exhibited, and *the signification of the term expressing it, learned in the only way in which it can be learned, through the senses, and by the aid of a sensible object.*

Federal Money.

31. The currency of the United States is called Federal Money. Its units are all denominate, being 1 mill, 1 cent, 1 dime, 1 dollar, 1 eagle. The law of change, in passing from one unit to another, is according to the scale of tens. Hence, this system of numbers may be treated, in all respects, as simple numbers, and indeed they are such, with the single exception that their units have different names.

They are generally read in the units of dollars,

How, if it be one of measure? What is the only way in which the idea of the unit can be acquired?

31. What is the currency of the United States called? Are its units simple or denominate? Name them. What is the scale, in passing from one unit to another? How, then, may this system of numbers be treated? In what respect do they differ from simple numbers? In what units are they generally read? How may the number $864,849 be read?

cents, and mills—a comma being placed after the figure denoting dollars. Thus,

$864,849

is read, eight hundred and sixty-four dollars, eighty-four cents, and nine mills; and if there were a figure after the 9, it would be read in decimals of the mill. The number may, however, be read in any other unit; as, 864849 mills; or, 86484 cents and 9 mills; or, 8648 dimes, 4 cents, and 9 mills; or, 86 eagles, 4 dollars, 84 cents, and 9 mills; and there are yet several other readings.

English Money.

32. The units of English, or Sterling Money, are 1 farthing, 1 penny, 1 shilling, and 1 pound.

The scale of this class of numbers is a varying scale. Its degrees, in passing from the unit of the lowest denomination to the highest, are, four, twelve, and twenty. For, four farthings make one penny, twelve pence one shilling, and twenty shillings one pound.

---

32. What are the units of English or Sterling money? Is the scale of this class of numbers constant or varying? What are its degrees in passing from the lowest to the highest unit?

Avoirdupois Weight.

33. The units of the Avoirdupois Weight are, 1 dram, 1 ounce, 1 pound, 1 quarter, 1 hundredweight, and 1 ton.

The scale of this class of numbers is a varying scale. Its degrees, in passing from the unit of the lowest denomination to the highest, are sixteen, sixteen, twenty-five, four, and twenty. For, sixteen drams make one ounce, sixteen ounces one pound, twenty-five pounds one quarter, four quarters one hundred, and twenty hundreds one ton.

Troy Weight.

34. The units of the Troy Weight are, 1 grain, 1 pennyweight, 1 ounce, and 1 pound.

The scale is a varying scale, and its degrees, in passing from the unit of the lowest denomination to the highest, are, twenty-four, twenty, and twelve.

---

33. What are the units of the Avoirdupois Weight? Is the scale constant or varying? What are the degrees of the scale in passing from the lowest unit to the highest?

34. What are the units of the Troy Weight? Is the scale varying or constant? What are the degrees of the scale in passing from the lowest unit to the highest?

Apothecaries' Weight.

35. The units of this weight are 1 grain, 1 scruple, 1 dram, 1 ounce, and 1 pound.

The scale is a varying scale. Its degrees, in passing from the unit of the lowest denomination to the highest, are, twenty, three, eight, and twelve.

Units of Measure.

36. There are three units of measure, each differing in *kind* from the other two. They are, Units of Length, Units of Surface, and Units of Solidity.

Units of Length.

37. The unit of length is used for measuring lines, either straight or curved. It is a straight line of a given length, and is often called the standard of the measurement.

---

35. What are the units of Apothecaries' Weight? How does the scale vary, in passing from the lowest unit to the highest?

36. How many units of measure are there? Name them.

37. For what is the unit of length used? What is the unit of length? What is it called? What gives the idea of the length of a line measured?

The units of length, generally used as standards, are 1 inch, 1 foot, 1 yard, 1 rod, 1 furlong, and 1 mile. The number of times which the unit, used as a standard, is taken, considered in connection with its value, gives the idea of the length of the line measured.

Units of Surface.

38. Units of surface are used for the measurement of the area or contents of whatever has the two dimensions of length and breadth. The unit of surface is a square described on the unit of length as a side. Thus, if the unit of length be 1 foot, the corresponding unit of surface will be 1 square foot; that is, a square constructed on 1 foot of length as a side.

1 square foot.

If the linear unit be 1 yard, the corresponding unit of surface will be 1 square yard. It will be seen from the figure, that although the linear yard contains the linear foot but three times, the square yard contains the square foot nine times. The square

1 yard.

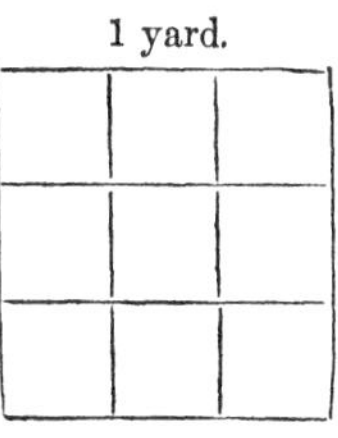

rod or square mile may also be used as the unit of surface.

The number of times which a surface contains its unit of measure, is its area or contents; and this number, taken in connection with the value of the unit, gives the idea of its extent.

Besides the units of surface already considered, there is another kind, called,

Duodecimal Units.

39. The duodecimal units are generally used in board measure, though they may be used in all superficial measurements, and also in solid.

The square foot is the basis of this class of units, and the others are deduced from it, by a descending scale of twelve.

---

38. For what are units of surface used? What is a unit of surface? If the unit of length be 1 foot, what will be the unit of surface? If the linear unit be a yard, what will be the unit of surface? How many times does the linear yard contain the linear foot? How many times does the square yard contain the square foot? What is a square rod? What is the area or contents of a surface? What gives an idea of its extent?

39. For what are the duodecimal units used? What is the basis of this class of units? How are the other units deduced from the basis?

40. It is proved in Geometry, that if the number of linear units in the base of a rectangle be multiplied by the number of linear units in the height, the numerical value of the product will be equal to the number of superficial units in the figure.

Knowing this fact, we often express it by saying, that "feet multiplied by feet give square feet," and "yards multiplied by yards give square yards." But as feet cannot be taken *feet times*, nor yards *yard times*, this language, rightly understood, is but a concise form of expression for the principle stated above.

With this understanding of the language, we say, that 1 foot in length multiplied by 1 foot in height, gives a square foot; and 4 feet in length multiplied by 3 feet in height, gives 12 square feet.

---

40. What principle, applicable to this subject, is proved in Geometry? How is this principle often expressed? Can we actually take a line a line times? When we speak of 1 foot in length multiplied by 1 foot in height, what do we mean? When we speak of 4 feet in length multiplied by 3 feet in height, what do we mean?

41. If, now, 1 foot in length be multiplied by 1 inch $= \frac{1}{12}$ of a foot in height, the product will be one-twelfth of a square foot; that is, *one-twelfth of the first unit:* if it be multiplied by 3 inches, the product will be three-twelfths of a square foot; and similarly for a multiplier of any number of inches.

If, now, we multiply 1 inch by 1 inch, the product may be represented by 1 square inch: that is, *by one-twelfth of the last unit.* Hence, *the units of this measure decrease according to the scale of* 12. The units are,

1st. Square feet—arising from multiplying feet by feet.

41. If 1 foot in length be multiplied by 1 inch, what will the product be? If it be multiplied by 3 inches, what will the product be? If we multiply 1 inch by 1 inch, what will the product be? What part is this of the preceding unit? According then to what scale do units of this measure decrease? What are the units of this measure?

2d. Twelfths of square feet—arising from multiplying feet by inches.

3d. Twelfths of twelfths—arising from multiplying inches by inches.

The same remarks apply to the smaller divisions of the foot, according to the scale of twelve.

The difficulty of computing in this measure arises from the changes in the units.

Units of Solidity.

42. It has already been stated, that if length be multiplied by breadth the product may be represented by units of surface. It is also proved, in Geometry, that if the length, breadth, and height of any regular solid body, of a square form, be multiplied together, the product may be represented by solid units whose number is equal to this product. Each solid unit is a cube con-

---

What is the scale? From what does the difficulty arise in computing by this measure?

42. If length be multiplied by length, what will be the unit of the product? What principle, applicable to this subject, is proved in Geometry? What is each solid unit? If the linear unit be 1 foot, what will the solid unit be?

structed on the linear unit as an edge. Thus, if the linear unit be 1 foot, the solid unit will be 1 cubic or solid foot; that is, a cube constructed on 1 foot as an edge: and if it be 1 yard, the unit will be 1 solid yard.

The three units, viz. the unit of length, the unit of surface, and the unit of solidity, are essentially different in kind. The first is a line of a known length; the second, a square of a known side; and the third, a solid, called a cube, of a known base and height. These are the units used in all kinds of measurement—excepting only the duodecimal system, which has already been explained.

Liquid Measure.

43. The units of Liquid Measure are 1 gill, 1 pint, 1 quart, 1 gallon, 1 barrel, 1 hogshead, 1 pipe, 1 tun. The scale is a varying scale. Its degrees, in passing from the unit of the lowest denomination are, four, two, four, thirty-one and a half, sixty-three, two, and two.

What three units are essentially different in kind? What is the first? What the second? What the third? Name all the kinds of units which are used in measurement.

43. What are the units of Liquid Measure? What are the degrees of the scale in passing from the lowest unit to the highest?

Dry Measure.

44. The units of this measure are, 1 pint, 1 quart, 1 peck, 1 bushel, and 1 chaldron. The degrees of the scale, in passing from units of the lowest denomination, are two, eight, four, and thirty-six.

Time.

45. The units of time are, 1 second, 1 minute, 1 hour, 1 day, 1 week, 1 month, 1 year, and 1 century. The degrees of the scale, in passing from units of the lowest denomination to the higher, are sixty, sixty, twenty-four, seven, four, twelve, and one hundred.

Circular Measure.

46. The units of this measure are, 1 second, 1 minute, 1 degree, 1 sign, 1 circle. The degrees of the scale, in passing from units of the lowest denomination to those of the higher, are sixty, sixty, thirty, and twelve.

---

44. What are the units of Dry Measure? What are the degrees of the scale in passing from the lowest unit to the highest?

45. What are the units of Time? What are the degrees of the scale in passing from the lowest unit to the highest?

46. What are the units of Circular Measure? What are the degrees of the scale in passing from the lowest unit to the highest?

Advantages of the System of Unities.

47. It may well be asked, if the method here adopted, of presenting the elementary principles of arithmetic, has any advantages over those now in general use. It is supposed to possess the following:

1st. The system of unities teaches an exact analysis of all numbers, and unfolds to the mind the different ways in which they are formed from the unit one, as a basis.

2d. Such an analysis enables the mind to form a definite and distinct idea of every number, by pointing out the relation between it and the unit from which it was derived.

3d. By presenting constantly to the mind the idea of the unit one, as the basis of all numbers, the mind is insensibly led to compare this unit with all the numbers which flow from it, and then it can the more easily compare those numbers with each other.

---

47. What is the first advantage named, which the system of separate units possesses over other systems, in presenting the elementary principles of arithmetic? What is the second? What the third? What the fourth?

4th. It affords a more satisfactory analysis, and a better understanding of the four ground rules, and indeed of all the operations of arithmetic, than any other method of presenting the subject.

The System of Units applied in the four ground Rules.

48. Let us take the two following examples in Addition, the one in simple and the other in denominate numbers, and then analyze the process of finding the sum in each.

SIMPLE NUMBERS.	DENOMINATE NUMBERS.				
	cwt.	*qr.*	*lb.*	*oz.*	*dr.*
874198					
36984	3	3	24	15	14
3641	6	3	23	14	8
914823	10	3	23	14	6

In both examples we begin by adding the units of the lowest denomination, and then, we *divide their sum by so many as make one of the denomination next higher.* We then set down the remainder, and add the quotient figure to the units of that denomination. Having done

48. Explain the common process in these two examples.

this, we apply a similar process to all the other denominations—*the principle being precisely the same in both examples.* We see, in these examples, an illustration of a general principle of addition, viz. *that units of the same kind are always added together.*

49. Let us take two similar examples in Subtraction.

SIMPLE NUMBERS.
8403
3298
5105

DENOMINATE NUMBERS.			
£	*s.*	*d.*	*far.*
6	9	7	2
3	10	8	4
2	18	10	2

In both examples we begin with the units of the lowest denomination, and as the number in the subtrahend is greater than in the place directly above, we suppose so many to be added in the minuend as make one unit of the next higher denomination. We then make the subtraction, and add 1 to the units of the subtrahend next higher, and proceed in a similar manner,

Is the principle employed, the same in both? What units are added together?

49. Explain the common process in these two examples.

through all the denominations. It is plain that the principle employed is the same in both examples. Also, that units of any denomination in the subtrahend are taken from those of the same denomination in the minuend.

50. Let us now take similar examples in Multiplication.

SIMPLE NUMBERS.

87464
5
437320

DENOMINATE NUMBERS.

℔	℥	ʒ	℈	*gr.*
9	7	6	2	15
				5
48	3	2	1	15

In these examples we see, that we multiply, in succession, each order of units in the multiplicand by the multiplier, and that we carry from one product to another, one for every so many as make one unit of the next higher denomination. The *principle* of the process is therefore the same in both examples.

51. Finally, let us take two similar examples in Division.

Is the principle employed the same or different? From what are units of any denomination subtracted?

50. Explain the common process in these two examples. Is the principle employed, the same in both?

SIMPLE NUMBERS.	DENOMINATE NUMBERS.			
	£	s.	d.	far.
3)874911	3)8	4	2	1
291637	2	14	8	3

We begin, in both examples, by dividing the units of the highest denomination. The unit of the quotient figure is the same as that of the dividend. We write this figure in its place, and then reduce the remainder to units of the next lower denomination. We then add in that denomination, and continue the division through all the denominations to the last—the principle being precisely the same in both examples.

---

51. Explain the common process in these two examples. Is the principle employed, the same in both ?

SECTION II.

FRACTIONAL UNITS.

Fractional Units which change according to the Scale of Tens.

52. If the unit 1 be divided into ten equal parts, each part is called *one tenth.* If one of these tenths be divided into ten equal parts each part is called *one hundredth.* If one of the hundredths be divided into ten equal parts, each part is called *one thousandth;* and corresponding names are given to similar parts, how far soever the divisions may be carried.

Now, although the tenths which arise from dividing the unit 1, are but equal parts of 1 they are, nevertheless, WHOLE tenths, and in this light may be regarded as *units.*

---

52. If the unit 1 be divided into ten equal parts, what is each part called? If one tenth be divided into ten equal parts, what is each part called? If one hundredth be divided into ten equal parts, what is each part called? Do similar names apply to all similar divisions? May these separate parts of one be regarded as entire units?

To avoid confusion, in the use of terms, we shall call every equal part of 1 a *fractional unit.* Hence, tenths, hundredths, thousandths, tenths of thousandths, &c. are *fractional units, each having a fixed relation to the unit* 1, from which it was derived.

53. Adopting a similar language to that used in integer numbers, we call the tenths, fractional units of the *first order;* the hundredths, fractional units of the *second order;* the thousandths, fractional units of the *third order;* and so on for the subsequent divisions.

Is there any arithmetical language by which these fractional units may be expressed? The decimal point, which is merely a dot, or period, indicates the division of the unit 1, according to the scale of tens. By the arithmetical language, the unit of the place next the point, on the right,

---

What is the general name for the whole class? Has each fractional unit a fixed relation with the unit 1?

53. What are the tenths called? What are the hundredths called? The thousandths? The tenths of thousandths?

Is there any arithmetical language to express these fractional units? What does the dot or period indicate? What is the unit of the place next to the dot on the right?

is 1 tenth; that of the second place, 1 hundredth; that of the third, 1 thousandth; that of the fourth, 1 ten thousandth; and so on for places still to the right.

The scale for decimals, therefore, is

.000000000, &c.;

in which the unit of each place is known as soon as we have learned the signification of the language.

If, therefore, we wish to express any of the parts into which the unit 1 may be divided, according to the scale of tens, we have simply to select from the alphabet, the figure that will express the *number* of parts, and then write it in the place corresponding to the *order of the unit.* Thus, to express four tenths, three thousandths, eight ten-thousandths, and six millionths, we write

.403806;

and similarly, for any decimal which can be named.

What is the unit of the next place? What is the unit of the next place?

What is the scale for decimals? What is known in regard to the places of this scale? What then is to be done when we wish to express any of the equal parts of the unit 1? Give an example of writing decimals.

54. It should be observed that while the units of place *decrease*, according to the scale of tens, from left to right, they *increase* according to the same scale, from right to left. *This is the same law of increase as that which connects the units of place in simple numbers.* Hence, simple numbers and decimals being formed according to the same law, may be written by the side of each other and treated as a single number, by merely preserving the separating or decimal point. Thus, 8974 and .67046 may be written

8974.67046;

since ten units, in the place of tenths, make the unit one in the place next to the left.

Fractional Units in general.

55. If the unit 1 be divided into two equal parts, each part is called a half. If it be divided into three equal parts, each part is called a third:

---

54. How do the units of place change their value from left to right? How do they change their value from right to left? How does this law compare with the law which exists in simple numbers? How then may simple and decimal numbers be written and treated?

55. If the unit 1 be divided into two equal parts, what is each part called?

if it be divided into four equal parts, each part is called a fourth: if into five equal parts, each part is called a fifth; and if into any number ot equal parts a name is given corresponding to the number of parts.

Now, although these halves, thirds, fourths, fifths, &c., are each but parts of the unit 1, they are, nevertheless, in *themselves,* whole things. That is, a half is a whole half; a third, a whole third; a fourth, a whole fourth; and the same for any other equal part of 1. In this sense, therefore, they are *units,* and we call them fractional units. Each is an exact part of the unit 1, and has a fixed relation to it.

56. Is there any arithmetical language by which these fractional units can be expressed?

The bar, written at the right, is the sign which denotes the division of the unit 1 into any number of equal parts. —

If it be divided into three equal parts, what is each part called? If into four, what is each part called? And if into any number of equal parts? How may these parts, in themselves, be regarded? How may a half be considered? A third? A fourth? And any other equal part of unity? What, then, may this class of numbers be called? Has each a fixed relation to the unit 1?

If we wish to express the number of equal parts into which it is divided, as 9 for example, we simply write the 9 under the bar, and then the phrase means, that some thing regarded as a whole, has been divided into 9 equal parts.

$$\overline{9}$$

If, now, we wish to express any number of these fractional units, as 7, for example, we place the 7 above the line, and read, seven ninths.

$$\frac{7}{9}$$

57. It was observed in Art. 7, that two things are necessary to the clear apprehension of an integer number.

1st. A distinct apprehension of the *unit* which forms the basis of the number; and

2dly. A distinct apprehension of the number of times which that unit is taken.

---

56. Is there any language for these fractional units? What does the simple bar denote? If you wish to express that the unit is divided into any number of equal parts, where do you write that number? If 9 be written under the bar, what does the phrase mean? If you wish to take or express any number of these fractional units, where do you write the number? If 7 be written above the line, what will the phrase then express?

57. How many things are necessary to the clear apprehension of an integer number? What are they?

Three things are necessary to the distinct apprehension of the value of any fraction, either decimal or vulgar.

1st. We must know the unit, or whole thing, from which the fraction was derived;

2d. We must know into how many equal parts that unit is divided; and

3dly. We must know how many such parts are taken in the expression.

The unit from which the fraction is derived, is called, the *unit of the fraction;* and one of the equal parts is called, the *unit of the expression.*

For example, to apprehend the value of the fraction $\frac{3}{7}$ of a pound avoirdupois, or $\frac{3}{7}$*lb.*; we must know

1st. What is meant by a pound;

2d. That it has been divided into seven equal parts; and

3d. That three of those parts are taken.

In the above fraction, 1 pound is the unit of the fraction; one-seventh of a pound, the unit of

---

How many things are necessary to the apprehension of a fraction? What are they? What is the unit from which the fraction is derived called? What is one of the equal parts called? Explain all that is necessary to apprehend the value of the fraction $\frac{3}{7}$ of a pound.

the expression; and 3 denotes that three fractional units are taken.

If the unit of a fraction be not named, it is taken to be the abstract unit 1.

Advantages of the System of Fractional Units.

58. By considering every equal part of unity as a unit of itself, having a certain relation to the unit 1, the mind is led to analyze a fraction, and thus to apprehend its precise signification.

Under this searching analysis, the mind at once seizes on the *unit of the fraction* as the principal basis. It then looks at the value of each part. It then inquires how many such parts are taken.

It having been shown that equal integer units can alone be added, it is readily seen that the same principle is equally applicable to fractional units; and then the inquiry is made: What is necessary in order to make such units equal?

If the unit of a fraction be not named, what unit is understood?

58. What is the first advantage named, of the system of fractional units? How does the mind analyze a fraction by the system of unities? What kind of integer units can be added together? Is the same principle applicable to fractional units?

It is seen at once, that two things are necessary:

1st. That they be parts of the *same unit;* and

2d. That they must be *like parts;* in other words, they must be of the same denomination, and have a common denominator.

In regard to Decimal Fractions, all that is necessary, is to observe that units of the same value are added to each other, and when written down, should always be placed in the same column.

59. The great difficulty in the management of fractions, consists in comparing them with each other, instead of constantly comparing them with the unity from which they are derived. By considering them as entire things, having a fixed relation to the unity which is their basis, they can be compared as readily as integer numbers; for, the mind is never at a loss when it apprehends the unit, the parts into

---

What is necessary in order that fractional units be equal to each other? What is to be observed in the addition of decimals?

59. In what does the great difficulty in managing fractions consist? What advantage do we get by considering them as entire things?

which it is divided, and the number of parts which are taken. The only reasons why we apprehend and handle integer numbers more readily than fractions, are,

1st. Because the unity forming the basis is always kept in view; and

2d. Because, in integer numbers, we have been taught to trace constantly the connection between the unity and the numbers which come from it; while in the methods of treating fractions, these important considerations have been neglected.

What are the reasons why we do not apprehend and manage fractions as easily as whole numbers?

SECTION III.

PROPORTION AND RATIO.

60. Proportion expresses the relation which one number bears to another, with respect to its being greater or less.

Two numbers may be compared, the one with the other, in two ways:

1st. With respect to their difference, called Arithmetical Proportion; and

2d. With respect to their quotient, called Geometrical Proportion.

Thus, if we compare the numbers 1 and 8, by their difference, we find that the second exceeds the first by 7: hence, their difference 7, *is the measure of their arithmetical proportion*, and is called, in the old books, their *arithmetical ratio.*

---

60. What is Proportion? In how many ways may numbers be compared together? What are those ways? If we compare the numbers 1 and 8 by their difference, what is the measure of their proportion? What is this measure called?

If we compare the same numbers by their quotient, we find that the second contains the first 8 times: hence, 8 is the *measure of their geometrical proportion,* and is called their *geometrical ratio.**

61. The two numbers which are thus compared, are called *terms.* The first is called the *antecedent,* and the second the *consequent.*

In comparing numbers with respect to their difference, the question is, *how much* is one greater than the other? Their difference affords the true answer, and is the measure of their proportion.

In comparing numbers with respect to their quotient, the question is, *how many times* is one greater or less than the other? Their quotient

* The term ratio, as now generally used, means the quotient arising from dividing one number by another. We shall use it only in this sense.

If we compare the same numbers by their quotient, what is the measure of their proportion? What is this measure called? In what sense is the term ratio now used?

61. What are the two numbers called which are compared together? When numbers are compared with respect to their difference, what question arises? What number affords the true answer? If numbers are compared with respect to their quotient, what is the question?

or ratio, is the true answer, and is the measure of their proportion. Ten, for example, is 9 greater than 1, if we compare the numbers one and ten by their difference. But if we compare them by their quotient, ten is said to be ten times as great—the language "ten times" having reference to the quotient, which is always taken as the measure of the relative value of two numbers so compared. Thus, when we say, that, the units of our common system of numbers increase in a tenfold ratio, we mean that they so increase that each succeeding unit shall contain the preceding one ten times. This is a convenient language to express a particular relation of two numbers, and is perfectly correct, when accurately defined.

62. All authors agree, that the measure of the geometrical proportion, between two numbers, is

---

What affords the true answer, and what does the quotient indicate? How much greater is ten than one, when we compare 1 and 10 by their difference? What do we say when we compare them by their quotient? To what has the language, ten times, reference? What do we mean when we say that the units in our common system of numbers increase in a tenfold ratio? For what idea is this a convenient language? Is it a correct language?

62. In what point do all authors agree?

their ratio; but they are by no means unanimous, nor does each always agree with himself, in the manner of determining this ratio. Some determine it, by dividing the first term by the second; others, by dividing the second term by the first.* All agree, that the *standard*, whatever it may be, should be made the divisor.

This leads us to inquire, whether the mind fixes most readily on the first or second number as a standard: that is, whether its tendency is to regard the second number as arising from the first, or the first as arising from the second.

63. All our ideas of numbers begin at one (Art. 1). This is the starting-point. We conceive of a number only by measuring it with one, as a standard. One is primarily in the mind before we acquire an idea of any other number. Hence, then, the comparison begins at one, which is the standard or unit, and all other numbers are measured by it. When, there-

* The Encyclopedia Metropolitana, a work distinguished by the excellence of its scientific articles, adopts the latter method.

In what respect do they differ? What are the two methods used, for determining the ratio? In what do they all agree? To what inquiry does this agreement lead?

fore, we inquire what is the relation of one to any other number, as eight, the idea presented is, how many times does eight contain the standard?

We measure by this standard, and the ratio is the result of the measurement. In this view of the case, the standard should be the first number named, and the ratio, the quotient of the second number divided by the first. Thus, the ratio of 2 to 6 would be expressed by 3, three being the number of times which 6 contains 2.

64. The reason for adopting this method of comparison will appear still stronger, if we take fractional numbers. Thus, if we seek the relation between one and one-half, the mind imme-

---

63. At what point do our ideas of numbers begin? How do we conceive of a number? What is primarily in the mind before we acquire an idea of any number? Where, then, does the comparison begin? When we inquire the relation between 1 and 8, what idea is suggested? What do we measure by? And what is the result of the measurement? In this view of the case, which should be the first number named? What the ratio? What is the ratio of 2 to 6? What does this show?

64. If we take fractional numbers, which method of comparison appears most natural? If we ask the relation between one and one-half, what does the mind first look to?

diately looks to the *part* which one-half is of one, and this is determined by dividing one-half by 1; that is, by dividing the second by the first: whereas, if we adopt the other method, we divide our standard, and find a quotient 2.

65. It may be proper here to observe, that while the term "geometrical proportion" is used to express the relation of two numbers, compared by their ratio, the term, "A geometrical proportion," is applied to four numbers, in which the ratio of the first to the second is the same as that of the third to the fourth. Thus,

2 : 4 :: 6 : 12,

is a geometrical proportion, of which the ratio is 2.

66. We will now state some further advantages which result from regarding the ratio as the quotient of the second term divided by the first.

Every question in the Rule of Three is a geometrical proportion, excepting only, that the

---

What number expresses the ratio? How is it found?

65. What does the term "geometrical proportion" express? What is meant by "A geometrical proportion?" What is the ratio of the proportion in the example?

last term is wanting. When that term is found, the geometrical proportion becomes complete. In all such proportions, the first term is used as the divisor. Further, for every question in the Rule of Three, we have this clear and simple solution: viz. that, the unknown term or answer, is equal to the third term multiplied by the ratio of the first two. This simple rule, for finding the fourth term, cannot be given, unless we define ratio to be the quotient of the second term divided by the first. Convenience, therefore, as well as general analogy, indicates this as the proper definition of the term ratio.

67. Again, all authors, so far as I have consulted them, are uniform in their definition of the ratio of a geometrical progression: viz. that it is the quotient which arises from dividing the second term by the first, or any other term by the preceding one. For example, in the progression

2 : 4 : 8 : 16 : 32 : 64, &c,

---

66. How may every question in the Rule of Three be regarded? Which term is used as a divisor in all such questions? What simole rule may then be given for finding the fourth term?

all concur, that the ratio is 2: that is, that it is the quotient which arises from dividing the second term by the first: or any other term by the preceding term. But a geometrical progression differs from a geometrical proportion only in this: in the former, the ratio of any two terms is the same; while in the latter, the ratio of the first and second is different from that of the second and third. There is, therefore, no essential difference in the two proportions.

Why, then, should we say that in the proportion

2 : 4 :: 6 : 12,

the ratio is the quotient of the first term divided by the second; while in the progression

2 : 4 : 8 : 16 : 32 : 64, &c.,

the ratio is defined to be the second term divided by the first, or of any term divided by the preceding term?

As far as I have examined, all the authors who have defined the ratio of two numbers to be the

67. In what definition are all authors uniform? What is that definition? Give an example. In what respect does a geometrical progression differ from a proportion? Is there, therefore, any essential difference?

quotient of the first divided by the second, have departed from that definition in the case of a geometrical progression. They have there, used the word ratio, to express the quotient of the second term divided by the first, and this without any explanation of a change in the definition.

Most of them have also departed from their definition, in informing us that "numbers increase from right to left in a tenfold ratio," in which the term ratio is used to denote the quotient of the second number divided by the first. The definition of ratio is thus departed from, and the idea of it becomes confused. Such discrepancies cannot but introduce confusion into the minds of learners. The same term should always be used in the same sense, and have but a single signification. Science does not permit the slightest departure from this rule. I have, therefore, adopted but a single signification of ratio, and have chosen that one to which all authors, so far as I know, have given their sanction; although some, it is true, have also used it in a different sense.

Is there, then, any reason for changing the signification of the term ratio?

68. One important remark on the subject of proportion is yet to be made. It is this:

Any two numbers which are compared together, either by their difference or quotient, must be of the same kind: that is, they must either have the same unit, as a basis, or be susceptible of reduction to the same unit.

For example, we can compare 2 pounds with 6 pounds: their difference is 4 pounds, and their ratio is the abstract number 3. We can also compare 2 feet with 8 yards: for, although the unit 1 foot is different from the unit 1 yard, still 8 yards are equal to 24 feet. Hence, the difference of the numbers is 22 feet, and their ratio the abstract number 12.

On the other hand, we cannot compare 2 dollars with 2 yards of cloth, for they are quantities of different kinds, not being susceptible of reduction to a common unit.

Simple or abstract numbers may always be compared, since they have a common unit 1.

---

68. What important remark is here made on the subject of proportion? Give an example. Can we compare two dollars with two yards? Can price and quantity be compared? May simple or abstract numbers always be compared? Why can they be compared?

SECTION IV.

APPLICATIONS OF THE SCIENCE OF ARITHMETIC.

69. Arithmetic is both a science and an art. It is a science in all that relates to the properties, laws, and proportions of numbers. The science consists in the examination and unfolding of these properties, and the investigation and development of the laws which regulate and govern all the operations that are performed on numbers.

70. Arithmetic is an art, in this: the science lays open the properties and laws of numbers, and furnishes certain principles from which practical and useful rules are formed, applicable in the mechanic arts and in business transactions. The art of Arithmetic consists in the judicious and skilful application of the principles of the

---

69. In what two lights may arithmetic be considered? In what is it a science? In what does the science consist?

70. What office does science perform? In what does the art of arithmetic consist? What do the rules contain?

science; and the rules contain the directions for such applications.

71. In explaining the science of Arithmetic, great care should be taken that the analysis of every question and the reasoning by which the principles are proved, be made according to the strictest rules of mathematical logic.

Every principle should be laid down and explained, not only with reference to its subsequent use and application in arithmetic, but also, *with reference to its connection with the entire mathematical science*—of which, arithmetic is the elementary branch.

72. That analysis of questions, therefore, where cost is compared with quantity, or quantity with cost, and which leads the mind of the learner to suppose that a ratio exists between quantities that have not a common unit, is, without explanation, certainly faulty as a process of science.

---

71. What caution is needed in explaining the science of arithmetic? How should every principle be dealt with? What is the elementary branch of mathematical science?

72. What is said of the analysis of those questions in which cost is compared with quantity, or quantity with cost?

For example: if two yards of cloth cost 4 dollars, what will 6 yards cost at the same rate?

Analysis.—Two yards of cloth will cost twice as much as 1 yard: therefore, if two yards of cloth cost 4 dollars, 1 yard will cost 2 dollars. Again: if 1 yard of cloth cost 2 dollars, 6 yards, being six times as much, will cost six times two dollars, or 12 dollars.

Now, this analysis is perfectly satisfactory to a child. He perceives a certain relation between 1 yard and 3 dollars, and between 4 yards and 12 dollars: indeed, in his mind, he *compares* these numbers together, and is perfectly satisfied with the result of the comparison.

Advancing in his mathematical course, however, he soon comes to the subject of proportions, treated as a science. He there finds, greatly to his surprise, that he cannot compare together numbers which have different units; and that his *antecedent* and *consequent* must be of the same kind. He thus learns that the whole system of analysis, based on the above method of

---

Give an example. Give the first analysis of this example. How does this analysis strike the mind of the pupil? What does he find in regard to it, when he comes to proportions?

comparison, is not in accordance with the principles of science.

What, then, is the true analysis? It is this: 6 yards of cloth being 3 times as great as 2 yards, will cost three times as much: but 2 yards cost 4 dollars; hence, 6 yards will cost 3 times 4, or 12 dollars. But if this last analysis be not as simple as the first, it is certainly more strictly scientific; and when once learned can be applied through the whole range of mathematical science.

73. There is yet another view of this question which removes, to a great degree, if not entirely, the objections to the first analysis. It is this:

The proportion between 1 yard of cloth and its cost, two dollars, cannot, it is true, as the units are now expressed, be measured by a ratio, according to the mathematical definition of a ratio. Still, however, between 1 and 2, *regarded as abstract numbers,* there is the same relation existing as between the numbers 6 and 12, also *regarded as abstract.* Now, by leaving out of

---

Give the true analysis. What is said of the last analysis?

73. What is said of another view of this question? Give that view.

view, for a moment, the units of the numbers, and finding 12 as an abstract number, and then assigning to it its proper unit, we have a correct analysis, as well as a correct result.

74. It should be borne in mind, that practical arithmetic, or arithmetic as an art, selects from all the principles of the science, the materials for the construction of its rules and the proofs of its methods. As a mere branch of practical knowledge, it cares nothing about the forms or methods of investigation—it demands the fruits of them all, in the most concentrated and practical form. Hence, the best rule of art, which is the one most easily applied, and which reaches the result by the shortest process, is not always constructed after those methods which science employs in the development of its principles.

For example, the definition of multiplication is, that it is the process of taking one number, called the multiplicand, as many times as there are

---

74. From what materials are the rules of practical arithmetic framed? Need a practical rule conform to the method of investigation which develops the principle on which it is based? What is the best rule of art? What is the definition of multiplication?

units in another called the multiplier. This definition, as one of science, requires two things.

1st. That the multiplier be an abstract number; and

2dly. That the product be of the same kind as the multiplicand.

These two principles are certainly correct, and applied to arithmetic as *a science*, are universally true. But are they universally true, in the sense in which they would be understood by learners, when applied to arithmetic as a mixed subject, that is, a science and an art? Such an application would certainly exclude a large class of practical rules, which are applied and used in the applications of arithmetic, without reference to particular units.

For example, if we have feet in length to be multiplied by feet in height, we must exclude the question as one to which arithmetic is not applicable; or else we must multiply, as indeed we do, without reference to the unit, and then assign a proper unit to the product.

What things does this definition require? In what point of view are these two principles true? What modifications must they undergo when applied to arithmetic as an art? Give the first example in which they must be modified.

If we have a product arising from the three factors of length, breadth, and thickness, the unit of the first product and the unit of the final product, will not only be different from each other, but both of them will be different from the unit of the given numbers. The unit of the given numbers will be a unit of length, the unit of the first product will be a square, and that of the final product, a cube.

75. Again, if we wish to find, by the best practical rule, the cost of 467 feet of boards at 30 cents per foot, we should multiply 467 by 30, and declare the cost to be 14010 cents, or $140,10.

Now, as a question of science, if you ask, can we multiply feet by cents? we answer, certainly not. If you again ask, is the result obtained right? we answer, yes. If you ask for the analysis, we give you the following:

1 foot of boards : 467 feet :: 30 cents : Answer.

Now, the ratio of 1 foot to 467 feet, is the ab-

Give the second example in which they must be modified.

75. Give the practical method of doing this example. As a question of science, can you multiply feet by cents? Is the ancwer found right? Give the analysis in full.

stract number 467; and 30 cents being multiplied by this number, gives for the product 14010 cents. But as the product of two numbers is numerically the same, whichever number be used as the multiplier, we know that 467 multiplied by 30, gives the same number of units as 30 multiplied by 467: hence, the first rule for finding the amount is correct.

76. I have given these illustrations to point out the difference between a process of scientific investigation and a practical rule.

The first should always present the ideas of the subject in their natural order and connection, while the other should point out the best way of obtaining a desired result. In the latter, the steps of the process may not conform to the order necessary for the investigation of principles; but the *correctness of the result* must be susceptible of rigorous proof. Much needless and unprofitable discussion has arisen on many of the processes of arithmetic, by confounding a principle of science with a rule of mere application.

---

76. What do these illustrations point out? How should the ideas be arranged in a scientific investigation? What is said about the formation of a rule of art?

SECTION V.

METHODS OF TEACHING ARITHMETIC CONSIDERED.

Order of the Subjects.

77. It has been well remarked by Cousin, the great French philosopher, that, "As is the method of a philosopher, so will be his system; and the adoption of a method decides the destiny of a philosophy."

What is said here of philosophy in general, is eminently true of the philosophy of mathematical science; and there is no branch of it to which the remark applies, with greater force, than to that of arithmetic. It is here, that the first notions of mathematical science are acquired. It is here, that the mind wakes up, as it were, to the consciousness of its reasoning powers. Here, it acquires the first knowledge of the abstract—separates, for the first time,

---

77. Repeat the remark of Cousin. Is this remark applicable to the philosophy of mathematical science? What is said of this remark, as applicable to the subject of arithmetic? What are the reasons given?

the pure ideal from the actual, and begins to reflect and reason on pure mental conceptions. It is, therefore, of the highest importance that these first thoughts be impressed on the mind in their natural and proper order, so as to strengthen and cultivate, at the same time, the faculties of apprehension, discrimination, and comparison, and also improve the yet higher faculty of logical induction.

78. The first point, then, in framing a course of arithmetical instruction, is to determine the method of presenting the subject. Is there any thing in the *nature* of the subject itself, and the connection of its parts, that points out the order in which these parts should be studied? Do the laws of science demand a particular order,—or are the parts so loosely connected, as to render it a matter of indifference where we begin and where we end? A review of the analysis of the subject will aid us in this inquiry.

79. We have seen (Art. 1) that the science of numbers is based on the unit 1. Indeed, the

---

78. What then is the first point in framing a course of mathematical instruction? What are the questions asked under this head? How are these inquiries to be aided?

whole science consists in explaining, illustrating, and developing the laws by which, and through which, we operate on this unit. There are three classes of operations performed on the unit one.

1st. To increase it according to certain scales, forming the classes of simple and denominate numbers:

2d. To divide it in any way we please, forming the decimal and vulgar fractions: and

3d. To compare it with all the numbers which come from it; and then those numbers with each other. This embraces proportions, of which the Rule of Three is the principal branch.

There is yet a fourth branch of arithmetic: viz. the application of the principles and of the rules drawn from them, in the mechanic arts, and in the ordinary transactions of business. This is called the Art, or practical part, of Arithmetic. (See Arithmetical Diagram facing the title-page.)

Now, if this analysis be correct, it establishes the order in which the subjects of arithmetic should be taught.

---

79. On what is the science of numbers based? In what does the science consist? How many classes of operations are performed on the unit one? What are they? If this analysis be correct, what does it establish?

Integer Units.

80. We begin first with the unit 1, and increase it according to the scale of tens, forming the common system of integer numbers. We then perform on these numbers the operations of the five ground rules: viz. numerate them, add them, subtract them, multiply and divide them.

We next increase the unit 1 according to the varying scales of the denominate numbers, and thus produce the system, called Denominate or Compound Numbers; after which we perform upon this class all the operations of the five ground rules.

REMARK.

81. It may be well to observe here, that the law of exact science requires us to treat the denominate numbers first, and the numbers of the common system afterwards; for, the com-

---

80. What is the first process in arithmetic? What is the second step? What is the second process? What is the next step?

81. What order does the law of exact science require, in treating the subject of arithmetic?

mon system is but a variety of the class of denominate numbers: viz. that variety, in which the scale is the scale of tens, and unvarying. But as *some knowledge of a subject must precede all generalization,* we are obliged to begin the subject of arithmetic with the simplest element.

Fractional Units.

82. We now pass to the second class of operations on the unit 1: viz. the divisions of it. Here we pursue the most general method, and divide it arbitrarily: that is, into any number of equal parts. We then observe that the division of it, according to the scale of tens, is but a particular case of the general law of division. We then perform on the fractional units, which thus arise, all the operations of the five ground rules.

Why does it require that order? Why do we not pursue this order?

82. What is the second class of operations on the unit 1? What method is here pursued? What do we first remark? What operations are then performed on the fractional units?

Comparison of Numbers, or Rule of Three.

83. Having considered the two subjects of integer and fractional units, we come next to the comparison of numbers with each other.

This branch of arithmetic develops all the relative properties of numbers, resulting from their inequality.

The method of arrangement, indicated above, presents all the operations of arithmetic in connection with the unit 1, which certainly forms the basis of the arithmetical science.

Besides, this arrangement draws a broad line between the science of arithmetic and its applications; a distinction which it is very important to make. The separation of the principles of a science from their applications, so that the learner shall clearly perceive what is theory and what

---

83. What subjects have already been considered? What subject comes next? What does this branch of arithmetic develop? In what connection does the method of arrangement adopted, present the subjects of arithmetic? What other advantages has this arrangement? Why is the separation of the science and applications of arithmetic an advantage?

practice, is of the highest importance. Teaching things separately, teaching them well, and pointing out their connections, are the golden rules of all successful instruction.

84. I had supposed, that the place of the Rule of Three, among the branches of arithmetic, had been fixed long since. But several authors, of late, have placed most of the practical subjects *before* this rule—giving precedence, for example, to the subjects of Percentage, Interest, Discount, Insurance, &c. It is not easy to discover the motive of this change. It is certain that the proportion and ratio of numbers are parts of the *science* of arithmetic; and the properties of numbers which they unfold, are indispensably necessary to a clear apprehension of the principles from which the practical rules are constructed.

We may, it is true, explain each example in Percentage, Interest, Discount, Insurance, &c. by a separate analysis. But this is a matter of much labor; and besides, does not conduct the

---

What are the golden rules of teaching?

84. In some later works on arithmetic, where has the Rule of Three been placed?

mind to any general principle, on which all the operations depend. Whereas, if the Rule of Three be explained, before entering on the practical subjects, it is a great aid and a powerful auxiliary in explaining and establishing all the practical rules. If the Rule of Three is to be learned at all, should it not rather precede than follow its applications? It is a great point, in instruction, to lay down a general principle, as early as possible, and then connect with it, and with each other, all the subordinate principles, with their applications, which flow from it.

Practical Part, or Applications of Arithmetic.

85. We come next to the 4th division; viz. the applications of arithmetic.

Under the classification which we have indicated, all the principles of the science will have been mastered, when the pupil reaches this stage

---

What are the reasons for placing the Rule of Three before the practical subjects? How may the difficulties be overcome? What are the objections to this method? What follows, if the Rule of Three precede the practical subjects? What is named as an important point in instruction?

85. What is the next subject to be considered? With what preparation does the pupil enter on this subject?

of his progress. His business will now be with the application of principles, and no longer in the study and development of the principles themselves. The unity and simplicity of this method of classification, may also be made more apparent, by the aid of the arithmetical diagram which faces the title-page.

May we not then conclude that the subjects of arithmetic should be presented in the following order:

1st. All the methods of treating integer numbers, whether formed from the unit 1 according to the scale of tens, or according to varying scales.

2d. All the methods of treating fractional unities, whether derived from the unit 1 according to the scale of tens, or according to the varying scales.

3d. The proportion and ratios of numbers; and

4th. The applications of the science of numbers to practical and useful objects.

In what does this subject differ from the science of arithmetic? Finally, then, in what order should the subjects of arithmetic be presented?

Objections to this Classification answered.

86. It has been urged that Common or Vulgar Fractions should be placed "immediately after Division, for *two reasons.*"

"First, they arise from division, being in fact *unexecuted* division."

"*Second,* in Reduction and the Compound Rules, it is often necessary to multiply and divide fractions, to add and subtract them, also to carry for them, unless perchance the examples are constructed for the *occasion,* and with *special reference* to *avoiding* these difficulties."

These, I believe, are all the objections that have been, or can be urged against the classification which I have suggested. I give them in full, because I wish the subject of arrangement to be fully considered and discussed. It should be our main object to get at the best possible system of classification, and not to waste our efforts in ingenious arguments in the support of a favorite one. We will consider these objections separately.

---

86. What different classification has been proposed? For what reasons? From what do fractions arise?

It is certainly true, that fractions "arise from division," but it is as certainly not true, that they are "*unexecuted* divisions," and this last idea has involved the subject in much mystery and difficulty.

The most elementary idea of a fraction, arises from the division of a single thing into two equal parts, each of which is called a half. Now, we get no idea of this half unless we consider the division *perfected*. And indeed, the method of teaching shows this. For, we cannot impress the idea of a half on the mind of a child, until we have actually divided in his presence the apple, (or something else regarded as a unit,) and exhibited the parts separately to his senses; and all other fractions must be learned by a like reference to the unit 1. Hence, we can form no notion of a fraction, except on the supposition of a *perfected division*.

If the term, "*unexecuted* division," applies to the numerator of the expression, and not to the unit of the fraction, the idea is still more involved. For, nothing is plainer than that we

---

Is the division executed or unexecuted? What is the most elementary idea of fractions? Do we get an idea of a half, before the division is finished? What does the method of teaching indicate? And what is the conclusion?

can form no distinct *notions of a result,* so long as the process on which it depends cannot be executed. The vague impression that there is something hanging about a fraction that cannot be *quite* reached, has involved the subject in a mysterious terror; and the boy approaches it with the same feeling which a mariner does a rocky and dangerous coast, of which he has neither map, nor chart, to guide him. But present to the mind of the pupil the distinct idea, that a fraction is one or more equal parts of unity, and that every such part is a *perfect whole,* having a certain relation to the thing from which it was derived, and all the mist is cleared away, and his mind divides the unit into any number of equal parts, with the same facility as the knife divides the apple.

The *form of expression* for a fraction, and for an *unexecuted* division, is indeed the same, but the interpretation of this expression, as used for one or the other, is entirely different. In our

---

What is said if the term "unexecuted division" be applied to the whole numerator? What difficulties result from not apprehending the nature of a fraction clearly? How does the form of a fractional expression compare with the expression which indicates an unexecuted division?

common language, the same word is not always the sign of the same idea, and in science, the same symbol often expresses very different things.

For example, $\frac{3}{7}$, as an expression in fractions, means, that something regarded as a whole has been divided in 7 equal parts, and that 3 of those parts are taken. As a result of division, it means that the integer number 3 is to be divided into 7 equal parts. Now, it cannot be assumed, as a self-evident fact, that three of the parts of the first division are equal to 1 part of the second; and if this fact be made the basis of a system of fractions, the mind of a child will go through that system in the dark. *The basis of every system should be an elementary idea.*

87. The second objection, as far as it goes, is valid. In all the tables of Denominate Numbers, fractions occur five times: viz. twice in Long Measure, where $5\frac{1}{2}$ yards make 1 rod,

---

Explain both and compare them. Can it be assumed that the two are equal? Can that idea be made the basis of a system of fractions? Why not?

87. What is said in regard to the second objection? How many times do fractions occur in the tables of denominate numbers?

and $69\frac{1}{2}$ statute miles 1 degree; once in Cloth Measure, where $2\frac{1}{4}$ inches make 1 nail; once in Square Measure, where $30\frac{1}{4}$ square yards make 1 square rod; and once in Wine Measure, where $31\frac{1}{2}$ gallons make 1 barrel. Now, it were a little better, if these tables had been constructed with integer units. But it should be borne in mind, that the first notions of fractions are given either by oral instruction, or learned from elementary arithmetics. Most of the leading arithmetics are, I believe, preceded by smaller works. These are designed to impart elementary ideas of numbers, so as not to *embarrass the classification of subjects when the scholar is able to enter on a system.* Now the most elementary of these works conducts the pupil, in fractions, far beyond the point necessary to understand and manage all the fractions which appear in the tables of denominate numbers: and hence, there is no reason, on that account, to depart from a classification otherwise desirable.

Where are the first notions of fractions generally taught? Why are the first notions of numbers so taught? What, then, weakens the force of the objection?

Objections to the Second Method considered.

88. Having examined the objections that have been urged against that system of classification of the subjects of arithmetic, which has appeared to me most in accordance with the principles of science, I shall now point out some of the difficulties to be met with in the adoption of the method proposed as a substitute.

1st. That method separates the simple and denominate numbers, which in their general formation differ from each other only in the scale by which we pass from one unit of value to another.

2d. By thus separating these numbers, it becomes more difficult to point out their connection and teach the important fact, that in all their general properties, and in all the operations to be performed upon them, they differ from each other in no important particular.

3d. By placing the denominate numbers after Vulgar Fractions, all the principles and rules are limited in their application to *a single class of fractions:* viz. to those fractions *which have the same unit.*

---

88. What is the first objection to the second method of classification? What is the second? What is the third?

For example, the common rule for addition of fractions, under this classification, is, in substance, the following: "*Reduce the fractions to a common denominator; add their numerators and place the sum over the common denominator.*"

As the subject of denominate numbers has not yet been reached, no allusion can be made to fractions having *different units*. If the learner should happen to understand the rule literally, he would conclude that, the sum of *all fractions* having a common denominator is found by simply adding their numerators and placing the sum over the common denominator. But this cannot, of course, be so, since $\frac{4}{9}$ of a £ and $\frac{5}{9}$ of a shilling make neither one pound nor one shilling.

What appears to me most objectionable in this method, is this: it fails to present the important fact, that no *two fractions* can be blended into one, either by addition or subtraction, unless they are parts of the *same unit*, as well as *like parts.*

By this method of classification most of the

What seems most objectionable in this method? What follows, in regard to examples, from the adoption of this method?

difficult questions which arise in fractions are avoided, or else the subject must be resumed after denominate numbers, and that class of questions treated separately.

The class of questions to which I refer, embraces examples like the following:

Add $\frac{5}{7}$ of a day, $\frac{4}{13}$ of an hour, and $\frac{3}{8}$ of a second together.

It is certainly true that a boy will make marvelous progress in the text-book, if you limit him to those examples in which the fractions have a common unit. But, will he ever understand the science of fractions unless his mind be steadily and always turned to the unit of the fraction, as the basis? Will he understand the value of one equal part, so as to compare and unite it with another equal part, unless he first apprehends, clearly, the units from which those parts were derived?

4th. By placing the Denominate Numbers between Vulgar and Decimal Fractions, the general subject of fractional arithmetic is broken

---

Give an example of the class of questions omitted. What is finally observed in regard to the effects of this method? What is the fourth objection to this classification?

into fragments. This arrangement makes it difficult to realize that these two systems of numbers differ from each other in no essential particular; that they are both formed from the unit one by the same process, with only a slight modification of the scale of division.

Simplicity and Generality of the Arithmetical Language.

89. We have seen that the arithmetic alphabet contains ten characters (Art. 11). From these elements the entire language is formed; and we now propose to show in how simple a manner.

The names of the ten characters are the first ten words of the language. If the unit 1 be added to each of the numbers from 1 to 10 inclusive, we find the first ten combinations in arithmetic (Art. 13). If 2 be added, in like manner, we have the second ten combinations: adding 3, gives us the third ten combinations, and

---

89. How many characters are there in the arithmetical alphabet? From what is the language formed? Explain the manner in which the first hundred combinations are formed. How many words did each new set of combinations introduce?

so on, until we have reached one hundred combinations (page 23).

Now, as we progressed, each set of combinations introduced one additional word, and the results of all the combinations are expressed by the words from two to twenty inclusive.

90. These one hundred elementary combinations, are all that need be committed to memory; for, every other is deduced from them. They are, in fact, but different spellings of the first nineteen words which follow one. If we extend the words to one hundred, and recollect that at one hundred, we begin to repeat the numbers, we see that we have but one hundred words to be remembered for addition; and of these, *all above ten are derivative.* To this number, must of course be added the few words which express the sums of the hundreds, thousands, &c.

91. In Subtraction, we also find one hundred

How many different words are necessary to express the results of these combinations?

90. What combinations is it necessary to remember? In what light may they be regarded? How many words are to be remembered for Addition? How many of these are derivative? What other words must be added to this number?

elementary combinations; the results of which are to be read (Art. 17). These results, and all the numbers employed in obtaining them, are expressed by twenty words.

92. In Multiplication, (the table being carried to twelve,) we have one hundred and forty-four elementary combinations (Art. 19), and fifty-nine separate words (already known) to express the results of these combinations.

93. In Division, also, we have one hundred and forty-four elementary combinations (Art. 20), but use only twelve words to express their results.

94. Thus, we have four hundred and eighty-eight elementary combinations. The results of these combinations are expressed by one hundred words: viz. nineteen in addition, ten in

---

91. How many elementary combinations are there in Subtraction? What is to be read in these? How many words are to be remembered?

92. How many elementary combinations in Multiplication? How many words to be remembered? Are they new words? Do they express new thoughts?

93. How many elementary combinations are there in Division? How many words will express the results of them?

subtraction, fifty-nine in multiplication, and twelve in division. Of the nineteen words which are employed to express the results of the combinations in addition, eight are again used to express similar results in subtraction. Of the fifty-nine which express the results of the combinations in multiplication, sixteen had been used to express similar results in addition, and one in subtraction; and the entire twelve, which express the results of the combinations in division, had been used to express results of previous combinations. Hence, the results of all the elementary combinations, in the four ground rules, are expressed by sixty-three different words; and they are the only words employed to translate these results from the arithmetical into our common language.

The language for fractional units *is similar*

---

94. How many elementary combinations are there in the four ground rules? By what are the results of these combinations expressed? How many words are used for this purpose in addition? In subtraction how many? How many in multiplication? In division how many? How many different words are used to express the results of the elementary combinations in the four ground rules? Is the language for fractional units the same? What is effected by means of a language thus formed?

in every particular. By means of a language thus formed we deduce every principle in the science of numbers.

95. Expressing these ideas and their combinations by figures, gives rise to the language of arithmetic. By the aid of this language we not only unfold the principles of the science, but are enabled to apply these principles to every question of a practical nature, involving the use of figures.

96. There is but one further idea to be presented: it is this,—that there are very few combinations made among the figures, which change, at all, their signification.

Selecting any two of the figures, as **3** and **5**, for example, we see at once that there are but three ways of writing them, that will at all change their signification.

First, write them by the side of each other - - - - - - - - - - - - - } **3 5**, **5 3**.

95. What constitutes the language of arithmetic? What is effected by the aid of this language?

96. Are there many or few combinations among the figures which change their signification?

Second, write them, the one over the other - - - - - - - - - - -	$\frac{3}{5}$, $\frac{5}{3}$.
Third, place a decimal point before each - - - - - - - - - - - . -	.3, .5.

Now, each manner of writing gives a different signification, to both the figures. Use, however, has established that signification, and we know it, as soon as we have learned the language.

We have thus explained what we mean by the arithmetical language. Its grammar embraces the names of its elementary signs, or Alphabet,—the formation and number of its words,—and the laws by which figures are connected for the purpose of expressing ideas. We feel that there is simplicity and beauty in this system, and hope it may be useful.

Necessity of exact Definitions and Terms.

97. The principles of every science are abstract ideas, having established connections with each other. In every branch of mathematics,

How many combinations are there, which change the signification of figures? Name and explain them in succession. Explain what is meant by the grammar of the arithmetical language.

the Definitions and Terms give form to, and are the signs of, certain elementary ideas, which are the basis of the science. Between any term and the idea which it is employed to express, the connection should be so intimate, that the one will always suggest the other.

These definitions and terms, when their significations are once fixed, must always be used in the same sense. The necessity of this is most urgent. For, *in the whole range of mathematical science there is no logical test of truth, but in a conformity of the reasoning to the definitions and terms, or to such principles as have been established from them.*

98. With these principles, as guides, we propose to examine some of the definitions and terms which have, heretofore, formed the basis of the arithmetical science. We shall not confine our quotations to a single author, and shall make only those which fairly exhibit the general use of the terms.

---

97. What is said of the principles of every science? What is said of definitions and terms? What is said of the relation between a term and its idea? What is said of conforming to the definitions and terms, when their significations are fixed? What reason is given?

It is said,

"*Number* signifies a *unit*, or a *collection of units.*"

"The common method of expressing numbers is by the *Arabic Notation.* The Arabic method employs the following *ten characters*, or *figures*," &c.

"The first nine are called *significant* figures, because each one always has a value, or denotes some number."

And a little further on, we have,

"The different values which figures have, are called *simple* and *local* values."

The definition of Number is clear and correct. It is a general term, comprehending all the phrases which are used, to express, either separately or in connection, one or more things of the same kind. So, likewise, the definition o: figures, that they are *characters*, is also right.

But mark how soon these definitions are departed from. The reason given why nine of the figures are called *significant* is, because "each one always has a value, or denotes some num-

98. Give the definition of number. State also how numbers are expressed. What is said of the definition of number? What is said of the definition of figures?

ber." This brings us directly to the question, whether a figure has a *value;* or, whether it is *a mere representative of value.* Is it a *number* or a *character* to represent number? Is it a *quantity* or *symbol?* It is defined to be *a character* which *stands for,* or expresses a number. Has it any other signification? How then can we say that it has a *value*—and how is it possible that it can have a *simple* and a *local value?* The *things* which the figures stand for, may change their value, but not the *figures themselves.* Indeed, it is very difficult for John to perceive how the figure 2, standing in the second place, is ten times as great as the same figure 2 standing in the first place on the right! although he will readily understand, when the arithmetical language is explained to him, that the UNIT of one of these places is ten times as great as that of the other.

99. Let us now examine the leading definition or principle which forms the basis of the arithmetical language. It is in these words:

Have figures value? What office, then, do they perform? Is the figure 2 any larger when it stands in the second, than when it stands in the first place?

"*Numbers increase from right to left in a tenfold ratio; that is, each removal of a figure one place towards the left, increases its value ten times.*"

Now, it must be remembered, that number has been defined as signifying "a unit, or a collection of units." How, then, can it have a *right hand*, or a *left?* and how can it *increase from right to left in a tenfold ratio?*" The explanation given, is, that "*each removal of a figure one place towards the left, increases its value ten times.*"

Number, signifying a collection of units, must necessarily increase according to the law by which these units are combined; and that law of increase, whatever it may be, has not the slightest connection with the *figures* which are used to express the numbers.

Besides, is the term *ratio*, (yet undefined,) one which expresses an elementary idea? And is the term, a "*tenfold ratio*," one of sufficient simplicity, for the basis of a system?

Does, then, this definition, which in substance

99. Repeat the principle which forms the basis of the arithmetical language? What objections are stated to the phraseology in which this principle is expressed?

is used by most authors, involve and carry to the mind of the young learner, the four leading ideas which form the basis of the arithmetical notation? viz.:

1st. That numbers are expressions for one or more things of the same kind.

2d. That numbers are expressed by certain characters called figures; and of which there are ten.

3d. That each figure always expresses as many units as its name imports, and no more.

4th. That the *kind* of thing which a figure expresses depends on the place which the figure occupies, or on the value of the units, indicated in some other way.

PLACE is merely *one* of the forms of language by which we designate the unit of a number, expressed by a figure. The definition attributes this property of place both to number and figures, while it belongs to neither.

100. Having considered the definitions and terms in the first division of Arithmetic, viz. in

---

What are the four leading ideas which form the basis of the arithmetical notation? What office does place perform? In what does the error of the definition consist?

Notation and Numeration, we will now pass to the second, viz. Addition.

The following are the definitions of Addition, taken from three standard works before me:

"The putting together of two or more numbers, (as in the foregoing examples,) so as to make one *whole number*, is called *Addition*, and the whole number is called the *sum*, or *amount*."

"ADDITION is the collecting of numbers together to find their sum."

"*The process of uniting two or more numbers together, so as to form one single number, is called* ADDITION."

"The *answer*, or the number thus found, is called the *sum*, or *amount*."

Now, is there in either of these definitions any test, or means of determining when the pupil gets the thing he seeks for, viz. the sum of two or more numbers?" No previous definition has been given, in either work, of the term SUM. How is the learner to know what he is seeking for, unless that thing be defined?

---

100. Give the different definitions of Addition. What objections are there to these definitions? How should Addition be defined?

Suppose that John be required to find the sum of the numbers 3 and 5, and pronounces it to be 10. How will you correct him, by showing that he has not conformed to the definitions and rules? You certainly cannot, because *you have established no test of a correct process.*

But, if you have previously defined SUM to be a number which *contains as many units* as there are in all the numbers added: or if you say,

"Addition is the process of uniting two or more numbers, *in such a way,* that all the units which they contain may be expressed by a single number, called the sum, or sum total;" you will then have a *test* for the correctness of the process of Addition: viz. Does the number, which you call the sum, contain as many units as there are in all the numbers added? The answer to this question will show that John is wrong.

101. I will now quote the definitions of Fractions from the same authors, and in the same order of reference.

---

101. Give the three definitions of fractions. What objection is stated to these definitions? What does the term fraction mean? What are the three prominent ideas concerning a fraction?

"We have seen, that numbers expressing *whole* things, are called *integers*, or *whole* numbers; but that, in division, it is often necessary to *divide* or *break* a whole thing into *parts*, and that these parts are called *fractions*, or *broken* numbers."

"Fractions are parts of an integer."

"*When a number or thing is divided into equal parts, these parts are called* FRACTIONS."

Now, will either of these definitions convey to the mind of a learner, a distinct and exact idea of a fraction?

The term "fraction," as used in Arithmetic, means one or more equal parts of something regarded as a whole: *the parts to be expressed in terms of the thing divided* CONSIDERED AS A UNIT. There are three prominent ideas which the mind must embrace:

1st. That the thing divided be regarded as a standard, or unity;

2d. That it be divided into equal parts;

3d. That the parts be expressed in terms of the thing divided, regarded as a unit.

These ideas are referred to in the latter part

Compare the three definitions separately, with these ideas.

of the first definition. Indeed, the definition would suggest them to any one acquainted with the subject, but not, we think, to a learner.

In the second definition, neither of them is hinted at. Take, for example, the integer number 12, and no one would say that any one part of this number, as 2, 4, or 6, is a fraction.

The third definition would be perfectly accurate, by inserting after the word "thing," the words, "regarded as a whole." It very clearly expresses the idea of equal parts, but does not present the idea strongly enough, that the thing divided must be regarded as unity, and that the parts must be expressed in terms of this unity.

102. I have thus given a few examples, illustrating the necessity of accurate definitions and terms. Nothing further need be added, except the remark, that they should always be used in the same sense, precisely, in which they are defined.

To some, perhaps, these distinctions may appear over-nice, and matters of little moment. It may be supposed that a general impression, im-

---

102. What is said generally of the advantage of accurate definitions and terms?

parted by a language reasonably accurate, will suffice very well; and that it is hardly worth while to pause and weigh words on a nicely-adjusted balance.

Any such notions, permit me to say, will lead to fatal errors in education.

It is in mathematical science alone that words are the signs of exact and clearly-defined ideas. It is here only that we can see, as it were, the very thoughts through the transparent words by which they are expressed. If the words of the definitions are not such as convey to the mind of the learner, the fundamental ideas of the science, he cannot reason upon these ideas; for, he does not apprehend them; and the great reasoning faculty, by which all the subsequent principles of mathematics are developed, is entirely unexercised (Art. 97).

It is not possible to cultivate the habit of accurate thinking, without the aid and use of exact language. No mental habit is more useful than that of tracing out the connection between ideas and language. In Arithmetic, that connection can be made strikingly apparent. Clear, distinct ideas—diamond thoughts—may be strung through the mind on the thread of science, and each have its word or phrase by which it can be transferred to the minds of others.

How should the subjects be presented?

103. Having considered the natural connection of the subjects of arithmetic with each other, as branches of a single science, based on a single unit; and having also explained the necessity of a perspicuous and accurate language; we come now to that important inquiry, How ought those subjects to be presented to the mind of a learner? Before answering this question, we should reflect, that two important objects should be sought after in the study of arithmetic:

1st. To train the mind to habits of clear, quick, and accurate thought—to teach it to apprehend distinctly—to discriminate closely—to judge truly—and to reason correctly: and

2d. To give, in abundance, that *practical* knowledge of the use of figures, in their various applications, which shall illustrate the stri-

103. What things have been previously considered? What question do we now come to? What is the first object to be sought for, in the study of arithmetic? What the second?

king fact, that *the art of arithmetic is the most important art of civilized life—being, in fact, the foundation of nearly all the others.*

Here a marked distinction should be observed between the Science and Art of arithmetic.

104. It is certainly true, that most, if not all the elementary notions, whether abstract or practical—that is, whether they relate to the science or to the art of arithmetic, must be made on the mind by means of sensible objects. Because of this fact, many have supposed that the *processes* of *reasoning* are all to be conducted by the same sensible objects; and that every abstract principle of science is to be established and developed by means of sofas, chairs, apples, and horses. There seems to be an impression that because blocks are useful aids in teaching the alphabet, that, *therefore* they can be used advantageously in reading Milton and Shakspeare. This error is akin to

---

What marked distinction, therefore, should be observed?

104. How are the elementary notions of arithmetic to be impressed on the mind? What mistakes have been made in regard to the processes of reasoning because of this fact? What impression seems to have existed? To what error is this akin?

that of attempting to teach practically, Geography and Surveying in connection with Geometry, by calling the angles of a rectangle, north, south, east, and west, instead of simply designating them by the letters A, B, C, and D.

This false idea, that every principle of science must be *learned practically*, instead of being *rendered practical by its applications*, has been highly detrimental both to science and art.

A mechanic, for example, knowing the height of his roof and the width of his building, wishes to cut his rafters to the proper length. If he calls to his aid the established, though *abstract principles* of science, he finds the length of his rafter by the well-known relation between the hypothenuse and the two sides of a right-angled triangle. If, however, he will learn nothing except *practically*, he must raise his rafter to the roof, measure it, and if it be too long cut it off, if too short, splice it. This is the practical way of *learning* things.

The truly practical way, is that in which skill is guided by science.

Do the principles above stated find any appli-

What false idea has prevailed? How has it operated?

cation in considering the question: How should arithmetic be taught? Certainly they do. If arithmetic be both a science and an art, it should be so taught and so learned.

105. The principles of every science are general and abstract truths. They are mere ideas, which we acquire through the senses by experience, or by processes of reflection and reasoning; and when acquired, are certain guides in every case to which they are applicable. If we choose to do without them we may. But is it wise to turn our heads from the guide-boards and explore every road that opens before us?

Now, in the study of arithmetic those principles of science, applicable to classes of cases, should always be taught at the earliest possible moment. The mind should never be forced

---

Give an example of the false practical. What is the true practical? Do the above principles find any application in considering how arithmetic should be taught?

105. What are the principles of every science? How do we acquire them? What is their use? When should the principles of science applicable to classes of cases be taught? Why? Should any examples precede a rule or the statement of an abstract principle? Why? Why should the learner not be carried forward through a series of them?

through a long series of examples, without explanation. One or two examples should always precede the statement of an abstract principle, or the laying down of a rule, so as to make the language of the principle or rule intelligible. But to carry the learner forward through a series of them, before the principle on which they depend has been examined and stated, is forcing the mind to advance mechanically—it is lifting up the rafter to measure it, when its exact length could be easily determined by a rule of science.

As most of the instruction in arithmetic must be given with the aid of books, we feel unable to do justice to this branch of the subject without submitting a few observations on the nature of text-books and the objects which they are intended to answer.

Text-Books.

106. A text-book should be an aid to the teacher in imparting instruction, and to the learner in acquiring knowledge.

It should present the subjects of knowledge in their proper order, with the branches of each subject classified, and the parts rightly arranged. No text-book, on a subject of general knowledge, can contain all that is known of the subject on which it treats; and ordinarily, it can contain but a very small part. Hence, the subjects to be presented, and the extent to which they are to be treated, are matters of nice discrimination and judgment, about which there must always be a diversity of opinion.

107. The subjects selected should be leading ones, and those best calculated to unfold, explain, and illustrate the principles of the science. They should be so presented as to lead the mind to analyze, discriminate, and classify; to see each principle separately, each in its combination with others, and all, as forming an harmonious whole. Too much care cannot be bestowed in forming the *suggestive method of arrangement:* that is, to place the ideas and

principles in such a connection, that *each step shall prepare the mind of the learner for the next in order.*

108. A text-book should be constructed for the purpose of furnishing the learner with the keys of knowledge. It should point out, explain, and illustrate by examples, the methods of investigating and examining subjects, but should leave the mind of the learner free from the restraints of minute detail. To fill a book with the analysis of simple questions, which any child can solve in his own way, is to constrain and force the mind at the very point where it is capable of self-action. To do that for a pupil, which he can do for himself, is most unwise.

109. A text-book on a subject of science should not be historical. At first, the minds of children are averse to whatever is abstract, because what is abstract demands thought, and thinking is mental labor from which untrained minds turn away. If the thread of science be broken by the presentation of facts, having no connection with the argument, the mind will leave the more rugged path of the reasoning and employ itself with what requires less effort and labor.

The optician, in his delicate experiments, excludes all light except the beam which he uses: so, the skilful teacher excludes all thoughts excepting those which he is most anxious to impress.

As a general rule, subject of course to some exceptions, but one method for each process should be given. The minds of learners should not be confused. If several methods are given, it becomes difficult to distinguish the reasonings applicable to each, and it requires much knowledge of a subject to compare different methods with each other.

110. It seems to be a settled opinion, both among authors and teachers, that the subject of arithmetic can be best presented by means of three separate works. For the sake of distinction, we will designate them the First, Second, and Third Arithmetics.

We will now explain what we suppose to be the proper construction of each book, and the object for which each should be designed.

First Arithmetic.

111. This book should give to the mind its first direction in mathematical science, and its first impulse in intellectual development. Hence, it is the most important book of the series. Here, the faculties of apprehension, discrimination, abstraction, classification, and comparison, are brought first into activity. Now, to cultivate and develop these faculties rightly, we must, at first, present every new idea by means of a sensible object, and then immediately drop the object and pass to the abstract thought.

We must also present the ideas consecutively: that is, in their proper order; and by the mere *method of presentation* awaken the comparative and reasoning faculties. Hence, every lesson should contain a given number of ideas. The ideas of each lesson, beginning with the first, should advance in regular gradation, and the lessons themselves should be regular steps in the progress and development of the arithmetical science.

112. The first lesson should merely contain the words placed opposite representations of sensible objects, to give the impression of their signification: thus,

One - - - - - - - *
Two - - - - - - - * *
Three - - - - - - - * * *
&c. &c.

And with young pupils, more striking objects should be substituted for the stars.

In the second lesson, the words should be replaced by the figures: thus,

1 - - - - - - -	*
2 - - - - - - -	* *
3 - - - - - - -	* * *
&c.	&c.

In the third lesson, I would combine the ideas of the first two, by placing the words and figures opposite each other: thus,

One - - -	1	Four - - -	4
Two - - -	2	Five - - -	5
Three - - -	3	Six - - -	6
&c.	&c.	&c.	&c.

The Roman method of representing numbers, making the fourth lesson, should next be taught: viz.,

One - - -	I.	Four - -	IV.
Two - - -	II.	Five - - -	V.
Three - -	III.	Six - - -	VI.
&c.	&c.	&c.	&c.

113. We come, now, to the first ten combinations of numbers, which should be given in a separate lesson. In teaching them, we must of course have the aid of sensible objects. We teach them thus:

One	and	one	are how many?
*		*	
One	and	two	are now many?
*		* *	
One	and	three	are how many?
*		* * *	
&c.		&c.	&c.

through all the combinations: after which, we pass to the abstract combinations, and ask, one and one, are how many? one and two, how many? one and three, &c.; after which we express the results in figures.

We would then teach in the same manner, in a separate lesson, the second ten combinations; then the third, fourth, fifth, sixth, seventh, eighth, ninth, and tenth. In the teaching of these combinations, only the words from one to twenty will have been used. We must then teach the combinations of which the results are expressed by the words from twenty to one hundred.

114. Having done this, in the way indicated, the learner sees at a glance, the basis on which

the system of common numbers is constructed. He distinguishes readily, the unit one from the unit ten, apprehends clearly how the second is derived from the first, and by comparing them together, comprehends their mutual relation.

Having sufficiently impressed on the mind of the learner, the important fact, that numbers are but expressions for one or more things of the same kind, the unit mark may be omitted in the combinations which follow.

115. With this single difference, the very same method should be used in teaching the one hundred combinations in subtraction, the one hundred and forty-four in multiplication, and the one hundred and forty-four in division.

When the elementary combinations of the four ground rules are thus taught, the learner looks back through a series of regular progression, in which every lesson forms an advancing step, and where all the ideas of each lesson have a mutual and intimate connection with each other. Will not such a system of teaching train the mind to the habit of regarding each idea separately—of tracing the connection between each new idea and those previously acquired—and of comparing thoughts with each other ?—and are not these among the great ends to be attained, by instruction ?

116. It has seemed to me of great importance to use figures in the very first exercises of arithmetic. Unless this be done, the operations must all be conducted by means of sounds, and the pupil is thus taught to regard sounds as the proper symbols of the arithmetical language. This habit of mind, once firmly fixed, cannot be easily eradicated; and when the figures are learned afterwards, they will not be regarded as the representatives of as many things as their names respectively import, but as the representatives merely of familiar sounds which have been before learned.

This would seem to account for the fact, about which, I believe, there is no difference of opinion: that a course of oral arithmetic, extending over the whole subject, without the aid and use of figures, is but a poor preparation for operations on the slate. It may, it is true, sharpen and strengthen the mind, and give it development; but does it give it that language and those habits of thought, which turn it into the pathways of science? The language of a science affords the tools by which the mind pries into its mysteries and digs up its hidden treasures. The language of arithmetic is formed from the ten figures. By their aid we measure the diameter of a spider's web, or the distance to the remotest planet which circles the heavens,—by their aid, we calculate the size of a grain of sand and the magnitude of the sun himself: should we then abandon a language so omnipotent, and attempt to teach arithmetic in one which is unknown in the higher departments of the science?

117. We come next to the question, how the subject of Fractions should be presented in an elementary work.

The simplest idea of a fraction comes from dividing the unit one into two equal parts. To ascertain if this idea is clearly apprehended, put the question, How many halves are there in one? The next question, and it is an important one, is this: How many halves are there in one and one-half? The next, How many halves in two? How many in two and a half? In three? Three and a half? and so on to twelve. You will thus evolve all the halves from the units of the numbers from one to twelve, inclusive. We stop here, because the multiplication table goes no further. These combinations should be embraced in the first lesson on fractions. That lesson, therefore, will teach the relation between the unit 1 and the halves, and point out how the latter are obtained from the former.

118. The second lesson should be the first, reversed. The first question is, How many whole things are there in two halves? Second, How many whole things in four halves? How many in eight? and so on to twenty-four halves, when we reach the extent of the division table. In this lesson you will have taught the pupil to pass back from the fractions to the unit from which they were derived.

119. You have thus taught the two fundamental principles of all the operations in fractions: viz.

1st. To deduce the fractional units from integer units; and

2dly. To deduce integer units from fractional units.

120. The next lesson should explain the law by which the thirds are derived from the units from 1 to 12 inclusive; and the following lesson

the manner of changing the thirds into integer units.

The next two lessons should exhibit the same operations performed on the fourth, the next two on the fifth, and so on to include the twelfth.

121. This method of treating the subject of fractions has many advantages:

1st. It points out, most distinctly, the relations between the unit 1 and the fractions which are derived from it.

2d. It points out clearly the methods of passing from the fractional to the integer units.

3d. It teaches the pupil to handle and combine the fractional units, as entire things.

4th. It reviews the pupil, thoroughly, through the multiplication and division tables.

5th. It awakens and stimulates the faculties of apprehension, comparison, and classification.

122. Besides the subjects already named, the First Arithmetic should also contain the tables of denominate numbers, and collections of simple examples, to be worked on the slate, under the direction of the teacher. It is not supposed that the mind of the pupil is sufficiently matured at

this stage of his progress to understand and work by rules.

123. In the First Arithmetic, therefore, should be taught,

1st. The language of figures;

2d. The four hundred and eighty-eight elementary combinations, and the words by which they are expressed;

3d. The main principles of Fractions;

4th. The tables of Denominate Numbers; and

5th. To perform upon the slate, the elementary operations in the four ground rules.

Second Arithmetic.

124. This arithmetic occupies a large space in the school education of the country. Many study it, who study no other. It should, therefore, be complete in itself. It should also be eminently practical; but it cannot be made so either by giving it the name, or by multiplying the examples.

125. The truly practical cannot be the antecedent, but must be the consequent of science. Hence, that general arrangement of subjects demanded by science, and already explained, must be rigorously followed.

But in the treatment of the subjects themselves, we are obliged, on account of the limited information of the learners, to adopt methods of teaching less general than we could desire.

126. We must here, again, begin with the unit one, and explain the general formation of the arithmetical language, and must also adhere rigidly to the method of introducing new principles or rules by means of sensible objects. This is most easily and successfully done either by an example or question, so constructed as to show the application of the principle or rule. Such questions or examples being used merely for the purpose of illustration, one or two will answer the purpose much better than twenty: for, if a large number be employed, they are regarded as examples for practice, and are lost sight of as illustrations. Besides, it confuses the mind to drag it through a long series of examples, before explaining the principles by which they are solved. One example, wrought under a principle or rule clearly apprehended, conveys to the mind more practical information, than a dozen wrought out as independent exercises. Let the principle precede the practice, in all cases, as soon as the information acquired will

permit. This is the golden rule both of art and morals.

127. The Second Arithmetic should embrace all the subjects necessary to a full view of the science of numbers; and should contain an abundance of examples to illustrate their practical applications. The reading of numbers, so much (though not too much) dwelt upon, is an invaluable aid in all practical operations.

By its aid, in addition, the eye runs up the columns and collects, in a moment, the sum of all the numbers. In subtraction, it glances at the figures and the result is immediately suggested. In multiplication, also, the sight of the figures brings to mind the result, and it is reached and expressed by one word instead of five. In short division, likewise, there is a corresponding saving of time by reading the results of the operations instead of spelling them. The method of reading should, therefore, be constantly practised, and none other allowed.

Third Arithmetic.

128. We have now reached the place where arithmetic may be taught as a science. The pupil, before entering on the subject as treated

here, should be able to perform, at least mechanically, the operations of the five ground rules.

Arithmetic is now to be looked at from an entirely different point of view. The great principles of generalization are now to be explained and applied.

Primarily, the general language of figures must be taught, and the striking fact must then be explained, that the construction of all integer numbers involves but a single principle, viz. *the law of change in passing from one unit to another.* The basis of all subsequent operations will thus have been laid.

129. Taking advantage of this general law which controls the formation of numbers, we bring all the operations of reduction under one single principle, viz. this law of change in the unities.

Passing to addition, we are equally surprised and delighted to find the same principle controlling all its operations, and that integer numbers of all kinds, whether simple or denominate, may be added under a single rule.

This view opens to the mind of the pupil a wide field of thought. It is the first illustration of the great advantage which arises from looking into the laws by which numbers are constructed. In subtraction, also, the same principle finds a similar application, and a simple rule containing but a few words is found applicable to all the classes of integer numbers.

In multiplication and division, the same striking results flow from the same cause: and thus this simple principle, viz. *the law of change in passing from one unit of value to another, is the key to all the operations in the four ground rules,* whether performed on simple or denominate numbers. Thus, all the elementary operations of arithmetic are linked to a single principle, and that one a *mere principle of arithmetical language.* Who can calculate the labor, intellectual and mechanical, which may be saved by a right application of this luminous principle?

130. It should be the design of a higher arithmetic to expand the mind of the learner over the whole science of numbers,—to illustrate the most important applications, and to make manifest the connection between the science and the art.

It will not answer these objects if the methods

of treating the subject are the same as in the elementary works, where science has to compromise with a want of intelligence. An elementary is not made a higher arithmetic, by merely transferring its definitions, its principles, and its rules into a larger book, in the same order and connection, and arranging under them an apparently new 'set of examples, though in fact constructed on precisely the same principles.

131. In the four ground rules, particularly, (where, in the elementary works, simple examples must necessarily be given, because here they are used both for illustration and practice,) the examples should take a wide range, and be so selected and combined as to show their common dependence on the same principle.

132. It being the leading design of a series of arithmetics to explain and illustrate the science and art of numbers, great care should be taken to treat all the subjects, as far as their different natures will permit, according to the same general methods. In passing from one book to another, every subject which has been fully and satisfactorily treated in the one, should be transferred to the other with the fewest possible alterations; so that a pupil shall not have to learn under a new dress that which he has already fully acquired. They who have studied the elementary work should, in the higher one, either omit the common subjects or pass them over rapidly in review.

The more enlarged and comprehensive views which should be given in the higher work will thus be acquired with the least possible labor, and the connection of the series clearly pointed out.

This use of those subjects, which have been fully treated in the elementary work is greatly preferable to the method of attempting to teach every thing anew: for there must necessarily be much that is common; and that which teaches no new principle, or indicates no new method of application, should be precisely the same in the higher work as in that which precedes it.

133. To vary the examples, in form, without changing in the least the principles on which they are worked, and to arrange a thousand such collections under the same set of rules and subject to the same laws of solution, may give a little more mechanical facility in the use of figures, but will add nothing to the stores of

arithmetical knowledge. Besides, it deludes the learner with the hope of advancement, and when he reaches the end of his higher arithmetic, he finds, to his amazement, that he has been conducted by the same guides over the same ground through a winding and devious way, made strange by fantastic drapery: whereas, if what was new had been classed by itself, and what was known clothed in its familiar dress, the subject would have been presented in an entirely different and brighter light.

CONCLUDING REMARKS.

134. I have thus completed, according to the plan which I proposed to myself, a full analysis of the language of figures, and of the construction of numbers.

We have traced from the unit one, all the numbers of arithmetic, whether integer or fractional, whether simple or denominate. We have indicated the laws by which they are derived from this common source, and pointed out the connections of each class with all the others.

We have also analyzed and explained that general, yet concise and beautiful language, by means of which numbers are made available in rendering the results of science practically useful.

We have also indicated our own impressions of the best methods of teaching this great subject—the foundation of all mathematical science—and the first among the useful arts: and an humble attempt to accomplish so good and great an object will, I am sure, be regarded with favor, even if the execution shall be found to fall far behind the importance and magnitude of the undertaking.

THE END.

www.ingramcontent.com/pod-product-compliance
Lightning Source LLC
LaVergne TN
LVHW021411110826
845150LV00007B/1872

9781425510923